THE AUTHOR

WENSLEY CLARKSON has written from inside the under-world for many years. He's encountered street gangsters with gunshot and knife wounds. He's met their wives and part-ners, some of whom have been kidnapped and attacked by rival street gangs. He's visited many such criminals in prison, received threats against his life from some and even attended a few of their post-mortems. Clarkson's books – published in more than thirty countries – have sold more than two million copies. He's also made numerous documentaries in the UK, US, Australia and Spain and written TV and movie screenplays. Clarkson's recent book *Sexy Beasts* – about the Hatton Garden raid – was nominated for a Crime Writers' Association Dagger Award.

www.wensleyclarkson.com

PRAISE FOR THE AUTHOR

THE REAL
TOP BOYS

The True Story of London's
Deadliest Street Gangs

WENSLEY CLARKSON

WELBECK

Published by Welbeck Non-Fiction Limited,
part of Welbeck Publishing Group.
20 Mortimer Street,
London W1T 3JW

First published by Welbeck in 2020

A CIP catalogue record for this book is available from the British Library

ISBN Paperback - 9781787395350

Typeset by seagulls.net
Printed and bound in the UK

10 9 8 7 6 5 4 3 2 1

www.welbeckpublishing.com

To the victims of street gangs, including the hard-pressed residents of the sprawling council estates that dominate London. You're not forgotten.

LONDON'S STREET GANG TERRITORIES

You're born, you take shit. You get out in the world, you take more shit. You climb a little higher, you take less shit. Till one day you've forgotten what shit even looks like.

XXXX, UNNAMED DRUG BARON STAR OF *LAYER CAKE*,
A FAVOURITE FILM OF LONDON RAPPER KANO,
WHO PLAYS SULLY IN *TOP BOY*

To make the big p's, the soldiers need to move up the ladder and become a top boy. That means buying in the shipments rather than selling the food on the streets. For many, it's the beginning of the end.

EAST LONDON STREET GANGSTER

*Just because we didn't lose…
doesn't mean we won.*

SULLY, *TOP BOY*

GLOSSARY
RULES OF THE GAME

These are the most used current London street words translated for those not "in the know". The rest you can work out for yourselves.

p's – money
brown – heroin
dubs and white – crack and coke
feds – police
snakes – informers
food – all drugs to sell
blud – friend

AUTHOR'S NOTE
KEEPING IT REAL

In *The Real Top Boys* I've tried not to glorify violence. However, this book has an obligation to reveal the harsh reality of street gangs across the mean streets of London.

My interest in the real top boys began long before the TV series existed. Back in 1992, I read Victor Headley's *Yardie*, a graphic crime novel about the trigger-happy gangsters who connected the drug worlds of London and Jamaica. It opened my eyes to a chilling netherworld and has intrigued me ever since.

Then, in 2008, I lived in a street of tightly packed terraced houses in Shepherd's Bush, west London, which contained a classic diverse mix of residents, as is so often the case in today's modern cities.

Many Caribbean families had moved there half a century ago. One neighbour asked me to speak to her thirteen-year-old son about the dangers of the underworld. He faced constant pressure from his peers to become a street gangster. I convinced this kid to avoid heading in that direction and we've been friends ever since.

I've been writing true crime books for more than thirty years and in that time I've met criminals of all shapes and sizes. But my encounters with some of the real street gangsters in this book were the most tricky.

They're virtually impossible to interview openly, so on some occasions I secretly tape-recorded their confessions. But that was a risky enterprise because many of them were clearly prone to violence. One so-called gangster got so paranoid, he pulled a knife on me before a friend dragged him off.

But the bravado shown by some of these young gangsters is nothing more than a front much of the time. Many of these kids are worn out, weary of what they're doing, but left with no choice but to carry on.

A lot of their friends are in prison. Others have died or been maimed. Very few of them ever make it out of the ghetto in one piece.

TWISTED DRAMA

When *Top Boy* first hit the small screen back in 2011, there were many raised eyebrows. Parents said the violence was too strong. Others dismissively said it made no commercial sense to screen a drama about a bunch of street gangsters, who had little in common with the rest of the population. How wrong they were.

What none of these critics 'got' was that the core of this TV series revolved around families and friends and relationships in a close-knit community immersed in danger, poverty and desperation.

Top Boy resonates with a much wider – and older – audience than one might expect, and many have come under the spell of the main characters, especially the psychotic killers among them!

From anti-hero top boy Dushane kissing teeth and occasionally talking in classic Jamaican patois, to his partner Sully's rolling walk, which says so much about his problematic life. These defining traits tell us so much about these characters and the life they lead.

Top Boy's television twist of reality has brought the mean streets of London to many of us who're supposed to abide by the law and live according to a set of rules designed to ensure our safety and protection.

But what happens when those same streets of London are overrun by real gangsters who only live for today? Bullets and blades fly in all directions and so often the innocent find themselves in the firing line.

THE WILD, WILD WEST

Mohanna Abdhou – known as Montana to her friends – was walking along a street towards the shops near her home. But the twenty-year-old was in the heart of gangster territory on the edge of a rundown South Kilburn housing estate: a concrete jungle ruled by a notorious street crew. She didn't even notice the two youths wearing bandanas riding near her on bicycles.

Moments later – as Montana continued strolling along that same stretch of pavement – a bullet ricocheted off a wall and hit her in the back, severing her pelvic artery. She died at the scene.

That bullet was later retrieved from Montana's body and a second was found in a nearby flat, although the revolver used in the shooting was never recovered.

The cold-blooded murder of Montana Abdhou highlights the random nature of London's street underworld. The Killy gang from that South Kilburn estate bordering the street where the killing took place had been in a long-running war with the Harrow Boys from the next-door Mozart Estate.

It was their bullet that killed innocent Montana following years of tit-for-tat violence about territories separated by a couple of streets. As one resident said just after the shooting: "This place was bad enough as it was. Now it feels like a war zone. We don't spend time outside in case one of our kids ends up dead like that poor girl."

One woman was later accused of assisting the alleged gunmen to evade capture in the hours following Montana's shooting. Another teenage boy even provided the alleged killers with the bikes and a place to change. This deadly real-life gang rivalry tragically mirrors the type of violence highlighted on TV's *Top Boy*.

For on the real streets and housing estates of London are more than two hundred gangs waging war. Their attacks have also included knifings, arson and numerous head injuries caused by vicious assaults.

In south London, at least fifty gangs "control" territories from Earlsfield in the south-west to Woolwich in the south-east. This includes a high density of gangs in and around Brixton, Camberwell and Peckham, which have made this area the most dangerous for knife crime in the country.

Gang members from 410 in Brixton and the Woolwich Boys in south-east London consistently issue warnings that they'll continue their street war and cannot see any end to the violence.

Other notorious south London gangs include Moscow17 in Kennington and the Ghetto Boys in Deptford. On the Elmington Estate in Camberwell, several gangs are at war, which has resulted in many brutal street attacks in that area. In Croydon – on the edge of south London – the 'CRO' gang are spread across much of the borough.

North of the River Thames, leafy middle-class Islington is now dominated by at least fifteen separate gangs, including the Bemerton Mandem, near King's Cross, and the Busy Blocks in former Labour leader Jeremy Corbyn's constituency in the north of the borough.

East London has at least sixty gangs, including the 8910 in Dagenham, 7th in Stratford, and the notorious London Fields and Homerton gangs. In the more affluent west of the capital, thirty-five gangs roam the streets day and night, including those much-feared Harrow Road Boys and their next-door arch enemies the Killy and the Southall gang.

Some gangs dominate entire areas, like the Wembley Tamils, who control a district between Wembley Central and Alperton stations in north-west London. Many of these gangs often use the same names as their favourite drill MCs. Others draw on postcodes or bus routes to come up with their titles. And the majority of attacks between rival gangs are carried out by so-called "feral" groups rather than one assailant.

In London, violence against strangers has even become known as "trespass" and is also described by street gangsters as "repping" your postcode. These types of attacks are seen as part and parcel of living in certain areas of the capital.

Those same gangs constantly spray graffiti signs on walls and advertising hoardings as warnings to rival gangs not to encroach on their territory, and to remind the local population that they rule those streets with blades and guns.

Drugs are responsible for virtually all of this. London has evolved into one of the most violent, cocaine fuelled "societies" in the Western world. The illicit drugs market in the UK capital and across the nation is worth £10 billion a year and cocaine is the premier "product".

There are at least half a dozen immensely wealthy crime bosses behind London's never-ending cocaine boom. They make their fortunes by anonymously "feeding" the real top boys and their street crews with all their food supplies.

Young gangsters similar to those featured on *Top Boy* thrive on housing estates all over London. No wonder the capital is the unrivalled epicentre of this entire subterranean criminal network.

But what is it about these sprawling estates that provokes such danger, violence and blatant criminality?

INTRODUCTION

CONCRETE JUNGLES

There is no future in these places. They make
you rot from the inside . No wonder the kids
turn to crime. What else can they do?

LONDON HOUSING ESTATE RESIDENT

THEM AND US

London's original housing estates were built almost one
hundred years ago to replace the capital's slums after the
First World War. People were given access to running
water, indoor toilets and private gardens for the first time.
These early estates were quickly dubbed "corned beef cities"
because it was presumed that the low-cost, low-quality
tinned meat was all people who lived on them could afford
to eat. It was this "them and us" attitude that soon made
many residents of these estates feel they'd been excluded
from so-called normal society.

Another wave of council estates in London were built from the 1950s to the 1970s following a housing extension plan by the then Labour government. And that's when so many of today's vast, ugly tower blocks were constructed. The intention was to provide essential housing for a wide cross section of people uprooted from city centres where they could no longer afford to live.

But back when *Top Boy* was nothing more than an idea in a creative TV writer's head a dozen years ago, youths were already being lured into gangs on those estates and it soon became "normal" to witness street crews selling drugs in the heart of these sprawling, rundown urban residences.

But what are these estates really like? And how have they been allowed to turn into these lawless centres of crime and retribution?

GHETTO BIRDS

I visited one such estate in east London to try and get a handle on how and why these gangs have evolved. It opened my eyes to a secret netherworld in its own semi-permanent state of lockdown. A place where crime thrives so much it has become the twisted heartbeat of the community.

Out of respect for its citizens, I haven't named this estate here. Many are ashamed of how their community has been overrun by street gangs. Others prefer to live in a state of semi-denial. Some are angry that they've been left to fend for themselves because the authorities seem to have stepped back from responsibility.

But there is no getting away from the fact that in this and so many other housing estates in London, many citizens are often afraid to venture out after dark.

Like so many estates in London, this one is modular, grey, cold and uninviting. Broken playgrounds. Litter scattered across scrubby, dog shit-infested grassland. A sense of hopelessness pervades the air. Crumbling nearby railway arches and a twisting tarmac-cracked flyover provide an unofficial border between this estate and the rest of the world. Subterranean networks of young gangsters loiter on the walkways and alleyways and those flashpoint inner-city roads that divide crew territories.

This particular estate stretches across twenty-five hectares and consists of a maze of walkways linking four dilapidated tower blocks. It's home to many thousands of people, who represent a vast cross section of London's population.

When a drone camera swoops high above them, it's clear to see the angry expressions on the faces of those same loitering gangs of youths in hoodies hunched up against the cold. A lot of residents here presume that the drones buzzing like insects are being remotely piloted by the police. They've all but given up going on foot patrols inside this and most other London estates. It's easier and safer to spy from the sky.

Very occasionally, a police patrol car pulls up on one of the streets that border this estate. Groups of loitering youths jeer and sneer at the feds and they drive off. The police have little appetite for confrontations with the locals round these parts.

Buying a loaf of bread from a corner shop can lead to a knife threat here. As one eleven-year-old resident explained to me: "They want p's. I had a quid my mum gave me to get some bread, so they took it. It's no big problem. This sorta thing happens all the time round here."

The same kid added: "If they say, 'gimme your phone or I shoot ya', ya just do it or they might push that gun in yer face and press the trigger."

A popular "job" for a lot of pre-teen kids on this and other London estates is to be "a spotter", which means floating around on BMX bikes watching out for the feds or invading rival gangs.

Kids who rode around housing estates a few years back have morphed into the chilling new generation of street gangsters providing *Top Boy* with much of its most potent dramatic inspiration.

Not surprisingly, youths on this estate live by their own "rules". As one former street gangster explained: "Here, everyone curses, a lot of girls sleep with men from thirteen or fourteen and often get pregnant. That life needs to be supported with quick money. There is no choice for many kids."

This estate in east London has all the signs of being a pressure cooker waiting to explode. Many of the kids hanging around on the walkways look angry and bored. Other residents avoid eye contact with them.

The first series of *Top Boy* featured a teenage girl holding guns in her family's flat for the local street gangsters. In real life, so many flats on estates like this one have their own dark, underworld secrets.

Another former street gangster told me: "You can get everything you want inside here. Even guns. They know how the system works inside these places. That means less chance of being caught by the feds or attacked by an enemy."

One law-abiding youth summed it all up: "If you're an innocent kid living here who doesn't want the gang life, then others will come after you to join them. They feel threatened by anyone who's not part of their 'club'."

No wonder the old residents here keep their doors tightly locked so much of the time.

MELTING POT

There's a small handful of original residents who've lived on this estate for more than forty years. They're mostly frail and elderly, so are unlikely to be out at night to see for themselves how this concrete jungle transforms into an open-air narcotics market as drug dealers emerge from the shadows.

Back when these now-elderly residents were young there were things to do. One explained: "You went to a youth club because it kept you off of street corners." But such amenities on this estate are long gone. In their place are fast food joints, local grocery stores and chain supermarkets, plus a lot of boarded-up shop fronts.

Children on housing estates like this one often feel disenfranchised. Boredom kicks in because there isn't much to do unless you join a gang. A love of sports often doesn't help either because many kids on estates cannot even safely walk half a mile to a sports hall or a football pitch in case they're attacked by a gang.

In recent times, new arrivals on this and other London estates have included Nigerians, Moroccans, Eastern Europeans, South Americans. This influx of immigrants was supposed to give these estates a new cultural identity. But recent reconstruction work on this particular estate had begun and then been hastily abandoned. It was to be part of a large-scale gentrification project. But today it's been left half-finished because the local council ran out of funds.

No wonder those who live here feel they are London's forgotten. Quite a few are unemployed and virtually penniless. A high number also have physical and mental health issues, as is so well highlighted in *Top Boy* series one.

Some flats on this estate have even been abandoned by residents evicted for non-payment of rent by the bankrupt local council, who can't afford to fix up these properties. So they're left to rot.

TRAP

Final port of call on my visit inside this east London housing estate is to one of those very same abandoned flats. I'm in the company of a former gangster, who still knows the street criminals who run the estate. They call this a "trap" for reasons that will soon become apparent.

It had been empty for many months until the local top boy and his street crew heard about it on the grapevine and moved in. Once inside, I'm introduced to that very same top boy. He's proud of his crew and immediately boasts how he never has less than three mobiles on him at any one time. One is for friends. The other is for family and the third one for business. But he often has at least two more burner phones for short-term work stuff.

Inside this once abandoned flat are at least ten unemployed teenagers cutting cocaine twelve to fifteen hours a day, often for minimum wages. This enables the street crew and their drug baron suppliers to earn at least five times more out of each shipment.

Teenage girls are chopping and sieving as if their lives depended on it. They don't wear any protective gear, not even latex gloves. The emphasis is on speed. They "step on" the cocaine by adding anything from baking powder to flour to it. Then it's tested just to make sure it still contains a slight hit, after which it's bagged up and the workers move on to the next bowl filled with white powder.

At the other end of this narcotics – "food" – conveyor belt are a couple of youths bagging up the final product in £20 and £10 plastic wraps. These are then thrown into two separate cardboard boxes ready to be handed over to the "*soldiers*", who will sell their produce through a small makeshift hole – or trap – cut out of the front door of this flat. Others will also soon be out selling drugs on the estate and surrounding streets.

This trap will probably close down within a few weeks, well before the police get to hear about it. Then another abandoned flat on a different part of the same estate will be taken over and the process will start all over again.

Meanwhile, young soldiers are out on the walkways, alleys and poorly lit surrounding streets, risking their lives and limbs in a dangerous narcotics netherworld where drug-addled customers and trigger-happy rivals are a constant threat.

The faceless drug barons – who supply the shipments of "food" now being sold on this estate and the surrounding streets – are pivotal to this and many other street gangs all over London.

These suppliers are tough, usually middle-aged characters who see all the death and destruction connected to London's street gangs as not their problem. They look on themselves as "businessmen"' and many come from long lines of professional criminals who've dominated London's crime scene for decades.

These same shady characters pull most of the strings whilst rarely getting their hands dirty. Like the ultimate evil sugar daddies (and mummies), they manipulate and intimidate the top boys and their crews with a combination of fear and brutality. They don't care who lives or dies. Everyone is expendable in their world.

Nothing, it seems, can quell the stench of violence committed in the name of drugs.

But where and how did London's explosion of narcotics, street crime and violence occur in the first place?

ACT 1

ORIGINAL GANGSTERS

You will get the money, me breddah,

when we get to your apartment.

YARDIE BY VICTOR HEADLEY

BACK IN THE DAY

There is undoubtedly a direct link between today's real *Top Boy* crews and the vicious gangs of criminals who dominated London's drugs underworld in the 1980s and 1990s.

Top Boy series three opened with estate crew boss Dushane living in Jamaica, having fled London after hitting back at a deadly gang of Albanian drug barons at the end of series two.

Dushane runs a car rental place in Jamaica, which is no doubt financed with his drug money from London. It seems as if Dushane's settled into a much quieter, more laid-back life in the Caribbean.

But looks can be deceptive. For Jamaica's real-life criminal hinterlands are riddled with more death and drugs than Dushane's old home back on *Top Boy*'s fictional Summerhouse Estate.

In Jamaica, Dushane – bored and in need of money – agrees to rob a post office with a local criminal. The heist never happens when Dushane and his one-eyed associate find the post office has closed down. But minutes later, Dushane has to shoot his partner in crime dead when he tries to rob an old granny in her grocery store instead. As a result, Dushane flees back to the UK capital to get away from deadly Caribbean gangsters and crooked local feds.

But then criminals like Dushane should know better. For the poverty-stricken slums of Jamaica's capital of Kingston are where a lot of the first really lethal drug gangs emerged more than four decades ago. They eventually headed further afield and helped fuel the Western world's toxic addiction to crack cocaine, which led – many years later – to the real top boys and the London drug wars that have inspired the hit TV series.

IN YER BLUD
KINGSTON, JAMAICA: 1970s

In the notorious slums of Trenchtown, the Jamaican government constructed housing developments built around large public courtyards, which were the hub of social and recreational activity in those rundown shantytowns.

In many ways, these blocks of flats with balconies were comparable to London's inner-city housing estates, which would later turn into deadly druglands for real street gangsters and their crews of dealers and henchmen.

But then Jamaica in the 1970s was already renowned in the Caribbean as a hideaway for criminals either on the run from the police or their enemies.

I stayed in a rundown motel in Kingston, in 1979, while working as a London crime reporter. In the middle of the night I heard loud voices in the room next door, which was only separated from me by an unlocked interconnecting door. The voices got louder and suddenly three gunshots rang out.

I lay there terrified, expecting the police to arrive, but no one came. Next morning, the manager of the hotel apologised for the disturbance and made it clear that the gangsters had left the premises. "Police no good, so we don't bother callin' them," he said in a matter-of-fact manner.

I realised then that some Jamaicans turned a blind eye to the criminals in their midst because it was safer for them. But unfortunately that attitude helped enable those gangsters to evolve into deadly forces.

By the end of the 1970s, Jamaica had become a mini narco-state version of what Mexico is today. The island was a pivotal transport hub for cocaine coming from South America en route to the US and then, later, the UK and Europe.

A large number of Jamaica's home-grown drug gangsters had friends and relatives living in the UK and US. They knew only too well that both those countries had a lot of cash to spend on narcotics. As a result, a lot of these chilling, cold-blooded criminals left their home country and soon became known to all and sundry as "Yardies".

THE YARDIES

The term comes originally from the Jamaican patois for people who frequented the "yard" of those two-storey con-crete homes built in Kingston's poverty-stricken ghettos.

In the UK, the term Yardie was initially used by the Caribbean expatriate and Jamaican diaspora community to refer to persons of Jamaican origin.

But then the word Yardie evolved into something more sinister: a term used for gangs or organised crime groups of Jamaican origin, nationality or ethnicity.

By this time, Jamaica's slums revolved around crime, drug abuse and violence. Crooked politicians even shamelessly bought and sold votes within these communities by paying gangs of Yardies to intimidate voters and threaten, assault or kill political opponents.

The parents and even the grandparents of some of the youths who've ended up in today's real street gangs in London arrived from the Caribbean in the 1950s and early 1960s. Back then, the British government encouraged West Indian residents specifically to help boost employment and productivity in post-war Britain. They brought with them their culture, food and music.

But by the late 1970s, the children from some of the poorer families had reacted against their strict upbringings and turned to gun crime and drug dealing, driven by the fast-emerging availability of crack cocaine. And naturally, their main suppliers of "food" came via the Caribbean homelands, especially Jamaica.

By this time, many of Kingston's poorest areas were daubed in gang graffiti that mentioned "heroic Yardies" and highlighted toxic territorial disputes. They became virtually no-go areas for the police, especially after dark.

However the police were also accused of wholesale violence and bribery. On Kingston's notorious Tulip Lane, locals clubbed together and formed protests against shootings by the police of local men.

But the feds insisted that all their "victims" were members of the city's drug gangs, who revelled in names such as the Scare Dem Gang, whose self-explanatory title was tagged across bridges and walls.

Homes belonging to gang members were sometimes daubed with new graffiti calling for the violence to stop. But most residents in these communities were too terrified to speak out against the Yardies, which enabled their underworld powerbase to continue to grow.

The main roads into Kingston's ghettos of Tivoli Gardens and Denham Town were regularly closed with police road blocks to try and stem the movement of gangsters. But nearby, the hustle and bustle of Coronation Market continued as thousands of Jamaicans from all across the island came to buy and sell produce.

Replace the rundown areas of Kingston with *Top Boy*'s Summerhouse Estate or any of the real-life concrete jungles of London and you start to get the picture. However, the side streets of the Jamaican ghettos were bleaker and more post-apocalyptic than even the baddest of housing estates back in London. I know because I visited them at the time as part of an investigation into drug running.

Women and children were frequently caught in the crossfire between Kingston's warring gangs at the time.

Pink Lane, in West Kingston, was and still is considered one of the most deadly street corners in the Jamaican underworld. Yardie gangs even fought with their rivals when they were living on the opposite side of the same road where they all resided.

By the end of the 1970s, Jamaican government budgets for drug prevention had been slashed. Political parties stopped paying money to gangs of unlawful armed supporters. So Yardie gangs concentrated even more on the drug trade.

Then the Jamaican government started cracking down so brutally on Yardie gangs that they literally drove many of them off the island. As a result, these hardened criminals arrived in the lucrative hinterlands of London and beyond.

The emergence of crack cocaine in both North America and the UK was to prove a goldmine for the Yardies. Up until this time, London's underworld had revolved around traditionally known crimes such as the Great Train Robbery and other heists which had dominated newspaper headlines for more than half a century. Then drugs began taking over.

Initially, some older home counties professional criminals tried to cash in on what they saw as a lucrative and safer alternative to robbing banks.

But then the Yardies emerged in large numbers in London. They already had connections to the Colombians via the Caribbean, which was at that time the main destination for cocaine en route from Latin America to the rest of the world. In London, they sought out UK underworld customers for vast shipments of cocaine. This initially led to an uneasy peace between the Jamaicans and the predominantly white old-school gangsters who ran London's drugs underworld at that time.

But the Yardies soon got greedy and decided to cut out the middlemen and set up their own distribution hubs in London and the rest of the UK. The old-time professional criminals quickly began retreating from the drug trade in fear of their lives.

The Yardies rapidly established strongholds in areas such as Brixton in south London, and Harlesden and Stonebridge in north-west London. They also began operating in the north and east London strongholds of Hackney and Tottenham.

The Yardies were building a cocaine and crack cocaine empire to feed London's entire drug market. In 1980, police seized 400kg of cocaine, a huge increase on the 80kg they'd recovered the previous year. A drug crime wave was enveloping the UK capital and the police had no idea how to stop it.

STOP AND SEARCH

The Yardies didn't hesitate to take out their gangster rivals in point-blank shotgun executions. So – as this drug-fuelled violence swept the streets of London – the body count skyrocketed and the police decided to take extreme measures to try and end this deadly lawlessness.

In 1980, London's Metropolitan Police set up the first of many specialist units to tackle the Yardies and their links with other Yardie gangs in the US. But it was an uphill struggle for the police because they knew so little about the Yardies themselves.

Then the London police secured draconian rights to stop and search anyone on the street they suspected of being involved in criminal activities. Inevitably, this was seen by many as an excuse for racism because the majority of people stopped under these newly introduced stop and search rules were black. As part of these new measures, officers were not even obliged to record the circumstances behind why an individual had been stopped.

Back in the early 1980s, drug dealing in London was much more fragmented. There were few specific street gangs. Instead, individual dealers had their street corners, which they closely guarded.

The days of full employment were long gone at this time and in the south London community of Brixton – where 25 per cent of residents were from ethnic minority groups – around half of young black men had no job. So a combination of high unemployment, deprivation, racial tensions and poor relations with the police began to be experienced by many across London and the UK's other main cities. One present-day street gangster explained: "My dad said back in the 1980s and 90s you got stopped by the feds every hundred yards in some places in London if you was black. No wonder we got resentful."

In the middle of all this, the police then launched Operation Swamp specifically to try and crack down on street crime in the south of the city. Officers stopped and searched vast numbers of young black men in Brixton. This sparked even more resentment, which threatened to boil over into outright violence towards the police.

Meanwhile London's Yardies were expertly feeding into the political and racial divide that was fast evolving in the UK's capital city. They were cashing in on a "perfect storm", which only they knew how to exploit.

By early April 1981, Operation Swamp had been branded a clumsy attempt by the police to try and cut street crime in Brixton. It had led to more than one thousand people in six days being stopped by police and undoubtedly ramped up Brixton's atmosphere of anger and suspicion against the feds. The area was like a tinderbox waiting to ignite.

KICKING OFF
BRIXTON: FRIDAY, 10 APRIL 1981

It was a typical Friday night in the bustling centre of this lively south London district. Many people were out on the streets and the pubs and clubs were heaving.

Then a local man called Michael Bailey was stabbed in a fight in one of those pubs. He ran out onto the street pleading for help, but was immediately bundled into a police car where he was held without medical attention. A crowd of young people pushed past police, pulled Bailey out of the officer's car and took him in a taxi to a local hospital.

Rumours soon swept Brixton that the feds had used outrageous brutality against Mr Bailey. This led to an angry crowd gathering in the centre of Brixton to confront officers. By the following day, thousands were out on the streets as word got out that the police had shown the man no mercy. It wasn't strictly speaking true but by then it didn't matter. Petrol bombs and missiles were hurled at the feds. Buildings and cars were set on fire and shops looted.

Teenage drug hoods were later alleged to have sparked armed battles between rival gangs for the most lucrative territories as the streets of Brixton became awash with blood, bullets and blades. Many who witnessed the riots insist that the relationship between the locals and the police back then was a lot worse than it is today.

One Brixton resident explained: "It felt as if the police hated us and couldn't care less about us. I remember one policeman saying near me once that the Brixton riots were good for the community because it meant the feds could crack down on us and keep us off the streets more."

One former south London police officer admitted: "A lot of police officers back then were white and racist. There is no point in denying it. We had a shameful attitude towards black people. It was them and us and we would use any weapon we could to keep them down."

None of this was helped by near-racist newspaper headlines, which were published to accompany reports of the riots. I know because I covered the riots as a young news reporter for a national newspaper back then. I was ashamed of some of that coverage at the time. And the scenes I witnessed have stayed with me ever since.

On day two of the riots, I watched a police officer on duty getting a beating from a crowd of youths. Riot police stepped back and allowed the beating to continue because they were so scared. Then dozens more riot police appeared as back-up and beat the shit out of the crowd.

"That sums up what it was like," explained one former Brixton resident. "We was blaming the police for everything but some of it was down to us also because we'd allowed our neighbourhoods to be controlled by drug dealers."

Many youths caught up in the Brixton riots later claimed to have suffered beatings at the hands of the police. Some of these were the fathers and even grandfathers of the top boys who are now running many of London's housing estates. One current Brixton resident explained: "My dad was caught up in the Brixton riots and he told us all about the feds and how they behaved back then. He convinced me that this country ain't a fair place for a black man, so you gotta take what you can."

From the Brixton riots in April 1981 up to July that year, there were more riots across the capital and in many other major UK cities. As a result of those disturbances, many streets and housing estates in north and south London turned into virtual no-go areas, where police now feared to tread. And throughout this period, the Yardies stepped up their drug dealing activities and consolidated their power and influence in these areas. After all, these were now prime, police-free locations to sell food.

The Yardies found it relatively easy to recruit disaffected, often unemployed local youths to distribute their drugs under the stewardship of mainly Jamaican bosses who wouldn't hesitate to have them killed if they stepped out of line or spoke to the feds.

ON THE GROUND

By early 1985, the Yardies had turned the Tottenham area of north London into their own personal feifdom. It was a much bigger district than Brixton and immersed in dire poverty, making it perfect territory for the Yardies to exploit.

These cold-blooded gangsters knew from their operations on the mean streets of Kingston, Jamaica, that slums were their most lucrative marketplaces. The demand for drugs was high in such places because narcotics helped deaden the pain of living on the breadline. Locals hated the police in these areas, so there was no danger they'd inform the feds about any gangsters in their midst.

Meanwhile, in that other notorious trouble spot of Brixton in south London, in September 1985 grandmother Cherry Groce was left paralysed from the waist down after she was shot by police officers looking for her son in connection with a robbery. Mrs Groce had to use a wheelchair until her death in April 2011 at the age of sixty-three. The jury inquest later blamed the Metropolitan Police for failures that contributed to Mrs Groce's death.

The police assault of Mrs Groce sparked a new round of riots in Brixton within days of the attack. This then spread to Liverpool's Toxteth area, Handsworth in Birmingham,

Chapeltown in Leeds, and Moss Side in Manchester. There were also less serious riots in other towns and cities.

Back in Tottenham, north London, one vast housing estate was on the verge of exploding. This particular concrete jungle – Broadwater Farm – was notorious as a lawless epicentre of drugs. Built in 1967, it contained more than a thousand flats, housing more than three thousand people. But by 1985, few police officers dared to patrol it. The Yardies and their young soldiers dominated the estate.

On 5 October that year a young man called Floyd Jarrett – who lived about a mile from the Farm – was arrested by police after being stopped in a vehicle with an allegedly suspicious car tax disc. He was taken to nearby Tottenham police station and charged with theft and assault (he was later acquitted of both charges).

Five and a half hours later, at 1 p.m., four police officers decided to search Jarrett's mother's home on the Broadwater Farm estate. Forty-nine-year-old Mrs Cynthia Jarrett was so upset when the police turned up, she collapsed and died from a heart attack.

During a later coroner's inquest into Mrs Jarrett's death, her daughter Patricia claimed to have seen one officer push her mother whilst conducting the search inside their house, causing her to fall. The policeman in question denied this allegation.

Within hours, Mrs Jarrett's death had sparked outrage among members of the black community against the conduct of the Metropolitan Police. There were widespread accusations that the police raid had been institutionally racist. The following day – 6 October 1985 – Mrs Jarrett's family met the police to discuss her death and demanded an inquiry. They made it clear they did not want any kind of public disorder.

A few hours later, at 6.45 p.m., police were called to disturbances on Mount Pleasant, Willan Road and The Avenue, which were all on the edge of the Broadwater Farm estate. When the feds arrived at the scene, they were immediately pelted with bottles and petrol bombs by an angry mob. Cars were then overturned and set alight alongside shops and other buildings. There was widespread looting.

Five hundred police with shields, helmets and truncheons then poured onto the streets and battled with rampaging youths as they threw bricks, bottles and cans from walkways inside the estate, as random fires turned the night sky red.

Nearby, PC Keith Blakelock was on foot patrol. He heard on his radio at 9.45 p.m. that several gunshots had been heard and one officer had been seriously wounded in nearby Griffin Road, so he headed towards the scene. At 10.15 p.m., PC Blakelock found himself surrounded by a mob of rioters. When they eventually dispersed, he was left crumpled on the pavement suffering from multiple stab wounds. PC Blakelock died later in hospital. Ten minutes after that stabbing, another officer was shot and slightly wounded. By midnight, a total of 58 policemen and 24 civilians had also been taken to hospital.

The Yardies believed the killing of a police officer was a major "victory" for them because it would make the feds even less likely to try and retain law and order on the estate. Stunned by the death of PC Blakelock and the earlier nation-wide riots, the police promised a more gentle approach to try and avoid all the racism accusations. But that was like further music to the ears of the Yardies, especially in London. Their foot soldiers were now operating with impunity on the inner-city streets and housing estates of the UK capital.

Then in the summer of 1986 – almost a year after the Broadwater Farm killing of PC Blakelock – the Yardies reminded London's drugs underworld that they were running things in emphatic, deadly fashion. Nigerian drug dealer Innocent Egbulefu made the grave mistake of selling fake cannabis to a Jamaican musician turned Yardie leader called Rankin Dread. The so-called drugs were actually made from herbs and tea leaves.

Egbulefu was in the toilet of his high-rise home in Islington, north London when Dread's associates smashed down the front door of his flat. Minutes later, Egbulefu plummeted ninety feet to his death while still grasping a television remote control. However the investigation into Egbulefu's death received little publicity at the time because the London police seemed uninterested in investigating the murder of black people, especially alleged drug dealers.

By the end of the 1980s, the Yardies were said to control at least 80 per cent of London's crack cocaine market and they now even had a reputation for carrying Uzi machine guns, which they'd use without hesitation on anyone who dared cross them. Meanwhile, across the Atlantic, street gangs often infiltrated by runaway Jamaican Yardies were winning their wars with the police and underworld rivals even more emphatically than the Yardies in London.

BOYZ N THE HOOD
LOS ANGELES, CALIFORNIA: 1990

A drug-fuelled gang war was raging on the west coast of America, which put a lot of the London underworld battles in the shade. Territory was the driving force behind an epidemic of deadly street violence that tainted LA's poverty-stricken South Central district during this time. There is no doubt that today's London's street gangs were greatly influenced by the crimelands of real Los Angeles during this period, epitomised by writer/director John Singleton's breakthrough movie *Boyz N the Hood*.

In those days, two chilling street gangs, The Crips and The Bloods, dominated the city's working-class black neighbourhoods from Compton to Long Beach. But there were no council housing estates in Los Angeles. It was and still is such a vast, sprawling city within an earthquake danger zone that tower block-style housing was not encouraged.

Instead, poor, low-rise neighbourhoods were connected by so-called grid street systems, which were similar to the way vast council housing estate were designed in the UK. These areas were dominated and "policed" by gangsters whose main income was derived from drugs. They protected their territories by "patrolling" them in gas-guzzling low rider cars.

"LA provided the template for many city street gangs across the world," explained one former Crip. "Movies like *Boyz N The Hood* made it clear that gangs could dominate neighbourhoods if they tightly controlled their territories."

From my interviews down the years with drug squad police officers in London and LA, I know that if a gang controls a specific territory, they can do whatever they want. The local population will rarely challenge them or tell the police about them because they know the gangsters will come looking. And when they do, it often ends in death.

DRIVE-BYS

Indiscriminate killings on the streets of LA in the 1980s and 1990s were usually classic drive-bys made popular by those same Crips and Bloods back then. These gangsters could strike at any time in any place they wished. Drive-bys also constantly threatened the safety of innocent bystanders.

The drive-by concept had been first developed as a form of retaliation in the late 1970s. Motorcycle ride-by killings were a common form of murder used by drug lord Griselda Blanco during her years controlling the Miami cocaine trade routes at that time. The drug underworld's favourite movie of all time, *Scarface*, starring Al Pacino, exposed the sheer brutality of those Latino gangsters in Miami as epitomised by Griselda Blanco. Blanco later herself died after being shot twice in the head by a motorcyclist in a drive-by shooting in Medellín, Colombia.

By the time LA's deadly race riots occurred in 1992, drive-bys on the streets of Los Angeles were an almost daily occurrence. These killings were considered the ultimate "hits" because they not only removed rivals but also sent out a message to the general population: *You will be killed if you cross us.*

Over on the east coast of the US, gangs of Yardies who'd originated in Jamaica had overrun New York City's drug trade in much the same way they'd done in London. One of the most deadly crews in the Big Apple was called The Shower People because the bullets from their Uzi machine guns showered people and they didn't care who got caught in the crossfire.

Around this time, New York police began introducing a so-called Zero Tolerance system when it came to street crime and it gradually helped to cut the amount of crime in the city. So a lot of Yardies quit New York and headed for London and other big UK cities. An even bigger crime invasion was in the pipeline.

LONDON'S TWISTED DRUGLANDS

In the UK capital, the police's highly controversial and racist stop and search powers were supposed to have been watered down after being blamed for provoking those streets riots in London and elsewhere throughout the 1980s. But all this did was further enable the Yardies to go from strength to strength. The rest of the London underworld looked on with terror because few other criminals were even prepared to challenge the Yardies' domination of the narcotics market.

Then in 1992, one of London's oldest crime families went on an unlikely recruitment drive and hired a much-feared Yardie gangster called Gilbert Wynter as a henchman. They were sending out a message to the Yardie drug lords running so much of London's drugs underworld at that time: "We're back."

Soon Gilbert Wynter was given pride of place at this same north London crime gang's "top table". Yardies in north and east London were outraged because they were convinced this move was a blatant attempt to outmuscle them from their prime territories in the UK capital.

Both sides went on a war footing. There were skirmishes and threats between gangsters from both camps. In one incident, Yardies were sprayed with bullets on a north London street. This all eventually culminated in a chilling face-off in a pub in Wembley, north-west London. But after guns were drawn, the crime family and the Yardies agreed an uneasy peace.

Shortly after this, Gilbert Wynter was arrested for the murder of a Yardie, who'd been executed after being called to a house in Stoke Newington, east London, to discuss claims that he was short-changing his drug suppliers, who happened to be the same north London family. It was rumoured that Wynter virtually sliced the Yardie in half with a Samurai sword. Wynter eventually walked free from London's Old Bailey criminal court after the main witness refused to give evidence. The judge condemned Wynter for being "a man who can commit this kind of crime and get away with it".

The Yardies then discovered that their former soldier Wynter had for many years been providing the family with invaluable inside information on Yardie operations. Wynter himself disappeared soon afterwards amid rumours that he'd actually been murdered by his own family bosses, who wanted to prove to their Yardie drug partners that they did not want a war.

Then in April 1993 in south-east London, black teenager Stephen Lawrence was murdered in cold blood by a gang of racist white youths as he waited at a bus stop. Once again, the police showed no real urge to find the killers. The Macpherson Inquiry into the murder of Stephen Lawrence later stated that all police stop and searches should be recorded in a bid to make them less forceful, although that recommendation wasn't actually implemented until April 2005. The police were, however, branded by Macpherson as institutionally racist.

The fallout from the cold-blooded murder of Stephen Lawrence provided yet another power vacuum for the Yardies. The police were so embarrassed by their failure to investigate the Lawrence murder properly that they had no choice but to further relax their stop and search activities.

But there had already been a complete breakdown of trust between the police and London's black population, and some areas of the capital had become no-go territories for law enforcement.

Then the Yardies brutally overstepped the mark, even by their standards.

CLAPHAM, SOUTH LONDON: 20 OCTOBER 1993

Reports of gunshots being heard in a residential area prompted PC Patrick Dunne to call at the home of a night-club security guard called William Danso. Within moments of arriving at the scene, PC Dunne had been shot in the chest by a man called Gary Nelson. He died shortly afterwards.

At Nelson's eventual trial many years later in 2006, it transpired that earlier that same night Nelson had been refused entry to a Brixton night club by Danso and there was a Yardie feud at the heart of the shooting. Nelson was sentenced to at least thirty-five years in jail.

Meanwhile, behind the scenes, the Yardies and their north London crime family "partners" continued their uneasy truce, thanks to the close friendship between one of their bosses and a Yardie posse chief. They'd once shared a cell in one of the UK's most high security prisons.

The same crime boss had even travelled to Jamaica to line up shipments of cocaine and cannabis through the Caribbean route from South America favoured by many drug smugglers at that time.

One of that crime boss's oldest associates later told me: "We were amazed he pulled it off and everything went much quieter for a while after that. The Yardies put their guns away and started making big money alongside us."

Then it all went pear-shaped again. One member of the same north London crime family cut the ear off the son of a Yardie gangster during a fight in a restaurant over some missing drug money. Days later, police raided the same Yardie gangster's house in north London and found a gun and a complete set of bullet-proof body armour. The Yardies suspected the north London family had stitched them up.

It was the mid-1990s and open warfare was then declared on the streets of London. Not surprisingly, the body count started to rise sharply. Grieving mothers began taking petitions to the then prime minister John Major at Downing Street to try and stop the murder and mayhem being committed by those in the London drugs underworld. Organisations such as Mothers Against Violence pushed a peace-first philosophy in the face of indiscriminate killings.

More and more family members found themselves literally caught in the crossfire. In the mid-1990s, one mother on a south London housing estate whose son was killed in gang violence was herself killed by another son, who never recovered from the psychological impact caused by the murder of his brother.

So all the warning signs were there, but neither the community nor London's law enforcement agencies seemed able to do anything to stem the violence.

KILLER POSSE

In spring 1998, London's law enforcement chiefs decided the only way to handle the capital's "Yardie problem" was to target the entire black population under the age of forty.

Scotland Yard launched Operation Trident specifically to investigate so-called black on black crime. It was a weak, ill-thought-out response to accusations that the police simply didn't care about crimes committed by black people on other black people. No wonder the Yardies were thriving in the middle of all this chaos.

At Scotland Yard, officers running Operation Trident tried to play down the racist undertones of their actions while many London residents were starting to say that the police simply didn't realise how anti-black they actually were.

The police defended themselves by claiming they were specifically targeting the Yardies, whom they said were involved in 40 per cent of the drug-related murders and attempted murders in London. Police identified twenty Yardie gangs, from six to twenty-strong, operating in the UK capital.

Then in June and July 1998, a gang of Yardies carried out three barbaric London murders, including the hitman-style execution of two young mothers. The Met police linked the slayings after forensic tests revealed the victims were killed with the same 9mm self-loading gun. Mums Avril Johnson and Michelle Carby had been shot in the head in their own homes. Their bullet-riddled corpses were discovered by their own kids.

The same Yardie posse then assassinated thirty-four-year-old Patrick Ferguson, inside his own home in Kingsbury, north London. It later emerged that each of the victims was linked to Yardie drug supply networks that ran right across London from Brixton to Stratford.

The Yardie hit squad had been utterly ruthless; they'd terrorised and even sexually assaulted their two female victims in a deliberate attempt to send a chilling message to their underworld rivals. "This sorta thing might happen in Kingston, Jamaica, or Cali, Colombia, even Harlem, but not London, for fuck's sake, " one old-time villain said at the time. "It's completely out of order. "

By that same year – 1998 – Yardie gun violence in London had escalated dramatically with a hundred and sixty murders in the capital. Forty-one victims were black and eighteen of those had been shot in classic Yardie-style hits. To put this into perspective, the black population of London comprised just 8 per cent of the entire city at that time.

Some old-school criminals were so shocked that they broke their own so-called code of honour and offered to help their historical enemies the police start trying to take down the Yardies.

One former bank robber explained: "Enough was enough. We had no choice. It had to be done if we were going to keep the streets safe and get everyone back in business."

One retired detective later recalled: "It was a very risky enterprise. Here we were in league with a bunch of hard-nosed old-school villains. Obviously it was never official policy and it was made absolutely clear that if anyone asked we would never admit to anything."

As a result, London's Yardie street gangs eventually pulled back from many of their street dealing activities. But they still had access to huge shipments of cocaine through contacts back in Colombia and the Caribbean.

However, the capital's drugs underworld was on the verge of big changes.

MELTDOWN

In the middle of all this, the issue of racism continued to haunt Scotland Yard when it came to dealing with the Yardies. Not only had the police unofficially joined forces with old-school gangsters but they were ignoring the basic rules when it came to dealing with London's drugs underworld. One former Yardie explained: "They couldn't stop us legally so the feds used those old racist white villains to try and destroy us."

One London-based modern-day street gangster later recalled: "I had an uncle who was a Yardie back in the day. They got him and put him away for twenty-five years. We had no doubt the judge gave him such a heavy sentence because he was black and that made us 'yungers' very angry.

"We wanted to get back at society for all this prejudice. I remember hearing one story on the estate where I lived about how a posse of three Yardies walked into a trap laid by the feds and two of them ended up being shot dead.

"It seemed to most of us that the racist feds were shooting down our brothers just because of the colour of their skin."

The Yardies' big mistake had been to try and conquer too much territory in their war with traditional London crime families. They should have just stuck to the specific London areas they knew and where they had complete control.

Meanwhile, some powerful Caribbean criminal names were mentioned in hushed tones inside the London homes of those with Yardie connections. These were households where such mobsters were the heroes who even featured in children's bedtime stories.

A rising name at this time was Christopher Michael Coke, known on the street as Dudus: a hyperactive Jamaican Yardie drug king who "worked" in both the Caribbean and London. Behind the scenes, Dudus was pulling more strings than any other Yardie in criminal history. He originated from Kingston and was proud of it. He was also brilliant at playing gangsters off against each other and always seemed to be one step ahead of the police.

Working alongside Dudus was a north London woman called Beverley "Bev" Storr, who'd later strike fear into a lot of criminals who operated inside the UK and European drug world.

Bev broke all the usual stereotypes. In an outrageously sexist era, she emerged as a crucial power player when it came to drug shipments coming in from the Caribbean. And both Bev and Dudus did not hesitate to flex their muscles when required.

CHICAGO NIGHTCLUB, PECKHAM, SOUTH-EAST LONDON: 31 JULY 2000, 2.50 a.m.

No one noticed the man in a passing car until he opened fire with an automatic machine gun at people queuing up to enter the nightclub for a late-night Jamaican music night event.

But few doubted the message the shooter was trying to send to the rest of the London underworld and Scotland Yard.

Dudas and Bev were rumoured to be behind the spree shooting. Nine customers were injured and the attack was seen as Dudus and Bev and their Yardie associates issuing a "statement" to their enemies.

"They wanted to terrify locals and get even bigger help-ings of respect from the drugs underworld," explained one former police detective from south London.

Back north of the river Thames, Bev Storr had fast estab-lished herself as the crime queen of one of Islington's most notorious housing estates. She was tall and hard-faced and had become the go-to drugs handler for up-and-coming street gangs. Dudus supplied much of the cocaine that Bev then sold on to the street gangsters under her control.

Bev had begun her criminal career smuggling shipments of cocaine and hash between Spain and Britain. In 1997 she'd been caught in Malaga with drugs worth £3 million and jailed for four years. Following her release in 2000, Bev returned briefly to Britain before going back to southern Spain's notorious Costa del Sol druglands. Then she suddenly quit the Mediterranean coastline and headed for a quiet village called Hou, in Denmark.

Bev turned her new home into an operations centre for the cocaine empire she ran in partnership with Dudus, who was smuggling huge quantities of food to Europe from the Caribbean. Bev even became the main intermediary between Colombia's Cali cartel and her underworld associates in London and the South-East of England. But her thirst for violence was growing.

A few weeks after arriving in Denmark, Bev turned up at a flat in the capital Copenhagen belonging to a British criminal called John McCormick, aged forty-seven. His terrified girlfriend was forced to watch McCormick being tortured and then shot dead by Bev. The girlfriend was too scared to ever reveal a description of the killer for fear of a reprisal.

McCormick – a convicted drugs smuggler from Liverpool – had originally fled to Scandinavia after "ripping off " a gang of British cocaine dealers in Spain. Police believed he was dealing cocaine at the time of his murder. He'd entered

Denmark from Spain the previous summer on a false passport in the name of Ronald Carey.

Meanwhile, Bev's biggest associate Dudus was secretly organising extra shipments of cocaine to sell on the side to other gangs in London and elsewhere. When he realised that Bev knew what he was up to, he ensured that their Colombian suppliers heard rumours that Bev was the one ripping them off.

As a result, the Cali cartel sent their European "manager" Arturo Miranda over from his base in Madrid to Denmark to pay Bev a visit. Miranda, fifty-four, disappeared shortly after arriving at Bev's house.

Later it emerged Bev and her live-in lover Reginald Blythin, fifty-five, from Chester, had shot and stabbed the Colombian and then dumped his body in a canal fifty miles north of Copenhagen. The corpse wasn't recovered until January 2001. Miranda had his hands tied behind his back. He'd clearly been tortured for hours before being killed.

Following Miranda's brutal murder, Bev Storr vanished from her cottage in Denmark. Neighbours later said they saw her hurriedly cleaning the house just before she disappeared. A police forensics team found traces of blood, leading detectives to conclude that Miranda's killing took place in the cottage before his body was dumped.

A few days later, Bev's red British-registered Volvo car was discovered abandoned at a railway station near the German border. She and her lover, Blythin, were immediately placed on Interpol's list of most wanted fugitives.

Back on Bev's old home turf of north London, there were rumours that a street gang boss who'd bought "food" from Bev had broken the underworld code of silence and informed on Bev to the police. He told detectives that Bev had been commissioned by white professional criminals to kill two members of the same street gang in revenge for a missing shipment of cocaine. There were also rumours that Bev's partner in crime Dudus Coke wanted her silenced.

In July 2002, Bev tried to board a flight at Schiphol airport, Amsterdam, using a fake Spanish passport. She was arrested after being surrounded by armed police acting on a tip-off. Police back in Denmark wanted to try Bev and Blythin together for the Miranda murder but he'd disappeared.

Following her arrest, Bev was flown back to Denmark under armed guard to face first-degree murder charges connected to the killing of Miranda. But instead of being kept in custody, Danish police requested that Bev be released on bail on the grounds they'd obtained all the information they needed from her. This was a ploy to get Bev to lead detectives to fellow suspect Blythin. But was it also a deliberate attempt to put Bev in the cross hairs of an underworld hit team?

However Bev survived – for the moment. The charges against her were thrown out and she eventually returned to the UK capital, moving into a flat in Newington Green Road, Islington, north London, close to the housing estate where she grew up.

Bev had a new boyfriend and linked up once again with Dudus, who was still providing shipments of drugs to be sold on to London street gangs. Bev organised taking over the corners on many local estates after the Yardies pulled away from "street duties".

But on Sunday 3 November 2002, Bev's new lover returned home late to find her lying dead in the living room of her flat. Local London feds who attended the scene insisted Bev's death was not suspicious. However they weren't aware of her criminal history. On the street, many were starting to say Bev had been killed in revenge for murdering that cartel man Miranda in Denmark.

Danish authorities believe to this day that Bev's medication may have been tampered with, or that she was forced to take an overdose to stop her from talking. Bev's criminal record and high-level connections with organised crime meant there were numerous gangsters keen to silence her. As the dust settled following Bev's death, most in the London underworld connected her demise to her onetime associate Dudus, whose criminal activities were rapidly turning him into one of the world's most wanted men.

Bev Storr's timely death undoubtedly helped Christopher "Dudus" Coke climb even higher up the global drugs ladder. By this time he was as big a fish in Jamaica as El Chapo would eventually become in Mexico.

NORTH LONDON: DECEMBER 2002

No doubt Dudus's legendary real-life story would have inspired TV top boy Dushane's decision to hide out in the

Caribbean, as he does in the opening episode of series three of the show.

Back in the real underworld, Dudus was at this time travelling between the Jamaican slums of West Kingston and specific Yardie strongholds in London using a vast array of false passports, yet hiding consistently in plain sight. Dudus's criminal activities in Jamaica eventually sparked a state of emergency on the island when police launched an operation aimed at trapping him. Prosecutors admitted that Dudus was so powerful he enjoyed "virtual immunity from the reach of law enforcement".

At the time, Dudus was even providing a safe haven for other Yardie members from Jamaica and the UK. He was also still sanctioning multiple crimes and drug deals. In Jamaica and certain parts of London, Dudus paid for the education and upkeep of many children in order to command the loyalty of local residents. He was so powerful and influential back in Jamaica that it would take authorities in the Caribbean years just to track him down.

In June 2010 Jamaican security forces – after many months of inexplicable delay – finally swooped on Dudus, mainly because the government at the time were under immense pressure from the UK and US governments to bring him to justice.

As the police surrounded Dudus's hideaway in West Kingston, he barricaded himself in his property. More than seventy people were killed as bullets flew in all directions from both sides during a fire fight that lasted ten hours. However, Dudus survived unscathed and was eventually extradited to the United States, where he was sentenced to a twenty-three-year prison sentence for drug and gun-trafficking.

LONDON: SUMMER 2010

Once Dudus had been removed from the marketplace, his relatives and rival criminals jostled for control of his underworld drugs empire. As a result, more than two hundred people were killed over a bloody two-year period and shipments of cocaine from the Caribbean slowed down significantly.

One local gang expert explained: "The gangs that operated out of certain areas of London by this time were not what I'd class as 'yardies', even if one or two may have been heavily influenced by that particular style of gangsterism.

"It was a hybrid culture. A mix of Jamaican, British and a dash of the American cultures. The Yardies' influence had been the brutality whereas the American influence was the flash aspect to it. The showing off the money, the jewellery, the cars, the materialism: that's all American."

Many of these fast emerging young gangsters had no direct connections to the countries where their parents and grandparents came from. They considered themselves British. Yet some of them would end up being deported to countries like Jamaica, which were essentially foreign to them.

Meanwhile, a few old-school British hoods came out of the woodwork claiming to be the street gangsters' friends and offering them cut-price deals for drug shipments. The street gangsters suspected that this food would be so heavily 'stepped on' that it wouldn't contain enough cocaine to actually hook in the customers.

However, it was clear that the pecking order – when it came to drug shipment suppliers – was changing virtually overnight. For these former bank robbers turned drug barons didn't trust street crews and vice versa.

"It was an uneasy peace," explained one former street gangster. "A lot of us thought the old-school criminals didn't respect us enough."

Some street gangsters became so suspicious of their new 'business partners' that they started carrying knives with them everywhere.

One former street gangster explained: "Underneath it we hated each other and the old British villains didn't like the way we was waving knives around, so they eventually began pulling back again."

Some of them retired and retreated from London to detached mansions deep in Kent and Essex while others cut their losses and headed for Spain and Thailand.

This left many London street gangs empty-handed – literally. Someone needed to step up to the plate and feed the city's insatiable demand for drugs.

IGNORING THE OBVIOUS

Back in the 1990s, most police officers hadn't seemed to really care about so-called "black on black" crime and this had definitely fuelled a war between gangsters, even when the brutal Yardies were running things.

Then around 2007 came a huge increase in the use of knives. By the next year there were 10,220 "knife-enabled crimes" in London but these figures were not openly published.

The following year – 2009 – London's Met Police even insisted that knife crime had dropped by nearly 20 per cent over the previous two years. But no one has ever been able to provide figures to back up those claims.

In 2010 a Youth Justice Board (YJB) survey reported a 12 per cent increase since 2002 in teenagers carrying weapons. The same survey saw a rise in violent crimes by fifteen and sixteen-year-olds, while Scotland Yard admitted that the murder rate for victims aged twenty and under trebled between 2005 and 2010.

The authorities in London already knew perfectly well by the start of the last decade that statistically a knife crime was being committed approximately every fifty minutes on the streets of the UK capital.

However, London's law enforcement agencies continued to take their foot off the pedal and as a result little was done to crack down on the increasingly prevalent use of knives.

One teenager called Bull from Edgware, north-west London, told me back in 2009 that he'd carried a knife from the age of nine because of bullies and gangs, and he claimed to have used it.

"I had no choice," he recalled. "This boy was taking the piss, so I stabbed him. Sure, I feel bad about it now but at the time it seemed like the only thing I could do."

Bull's victim was one of the lucky ones because he survived despite being badly injured. Bull then ended up attending a weapons workshop.

He explained: "That taught me about the damage a knife can do. We saw pictures of knife wounds. One showed if you stab someone in the stomach their intestines could fall out."

Bull stopped carrying a knife and today he's got a "real job" and doesn't live on an estate any more. However he's one of the lucky ones.

As Bull explained: "Most of my mates carried on using knives. It gave them big respect on the estates and the crews like that. But then they couldn't get work nowhere else."

Then something happened which was completely out of the hands of every gangster in London.

Part of the city once again went up in flames.

FERRY LANE, TOTTENHAM, NORTH LONDON: 4 AUGUST 2011, 6.15 p.m.

Rush hour on one of the capital's busiest streets. Few would have noticed the unmarked police cars shadowing a minicab, except passenger Mr Mark Duggan. He even texted his girl-friend to say the feds were following him.

Moments later, armed officers from both cars surrounded the mini-cab and ordered Mr Duggan to get out. They later claimed they'd received intelligence that he was armed.

The passenger door swung open and Mr Duggan – it was later alleged – pivoted out of the vehicle and tried to make a run for it. One firearms officer later stated he fired several shots after "seeing Mr Duggan raise a 'gun-shaped item in a sock' in his direction".

Police insisted they shouted at him to put down the weapon before firing.

Mr Duggan was pronounced dead a few minutes later and police insisted they located a firearm on a grass area less than five metres from his body.

But even the most battle-weary of local residents were shocked when they heard about the police shooting of local criminal Mark "Starrish" Duggan that summer's afternoon in 2011.

Some later alleged that trigger-happy police officers had been indiscriminately "culling" black gangsters on the streets of London for decades. In the third series of *Top Boy*, on-the-run psycho criminal Modie is mowed down by police bullets after his car is stopped by heavily armed feds in a busy street.

Top Boy star Kano – who plays Sully – has clearly implied that the real-life shooting by the police of criminal Mr Duggan was not only one of the inspirations for that dramatic scene in the series, but it also changed the real face of London street gangsterdom for ever.

The day after Mr Duggan died in a hail of police bullets a peaceful protest against the shooting was held outside the local police station on the Tottenham High Road, with three hundred demonstrators demanding "justice".

However this quickly turned into riots and looting, which eventually spread right across north London and beyond. Petrol bombs were thrown at the feds and patrol cars and buildings were set alight. Injured civilians and police officers were taken to hospital, some of them with serious head trauma.

The next night, there were other disturbances elsewhere in London, including Brixton, Enfield, Islington, Wood Green and in Oxford Circus in the heart of central London.

Twenty-four hours later – on Monday 8 August – problems flared up again in some areas of London. A man was found shot in Croydon, south London, and died later in hospital. Another man – who'd been assaulted in Ealing, west London – died in hospital.

Meanwhile, riots had flared up as far afield as Birmingham, Bristol, Gillingham and Nottingham, parts of the West Midlands and Manchester and Merseyside in the north-west of England.

Shots were fired at the police, including at a police helicopter. Petrol bombs were also thrown at officers. Three men were killed in Birmingham in a hit-and-run incident connected directly to the disturbances.

By the time all the disturbances had been quelled on 10 August 2011, at least 3,000 arrests had been made across England. More than a thousand people faced criminal charges for various offences related to the riots. Overwhelmed courts sat for extended hours. A total of 3,443 crimes across London were directly linked to the disturbances and at least £200 million' worth of property was damaged.

The 2011 riots that began in Tottenham and then spread across the UK, combined with the earlier incarceration of Dudus Coke, had a huge impact on London's drugs underworld.

The street gangsters of the previous decade who'd mainly worked for the Yardies and then briefly for the old-school criminals all but disappeared as supplies of drugs ran low. And the feds also began clamping down much harder on so-called "problem estates" in London following the riots.

A void was opening up in London's drugs underworld. But who would have the courage to fill it and cash in on the most lucrative drugs marketplace in Europe?

ACT 2

THE REAL TOP BOYS' WORLD

What's the point? Some blud could walk round the corner and shoot me in the head and I be dead before I reached the floor. Much better to live for today.

STREET GANGSTER DANIMAL

KILL OR BE KILLED

A new breed of street gangsters emerged on London's most notorious council housing estates following the Tottenham riots and they were even more cold blooded than their predecessors, who'd worked for the Yardies.

They seemed to have one simple premise: either kill or be killed.

At the centre of this chilling new netherworld of crime were top boys – often still in their teens – and their older drug-supplying paymasters. And this lethal combination began operating right on the doorstep of millions of law-abiding citizens.

BEST OF BOTH WORLDS

The gentrification of London in recent years has resulted in some of the most notorious housing estates bordering streets lined with million-pound-plus properties. The usual social and wealth dividing lines have become increasingly blurred.

As a result, the thriving metropolis began unintentionally camouflaging the underworld activities of some of the most dangerous gangsters this country has ever seen.

I first met Patrick more than ten years ago through a contact in east London. On the surface, he seemed a highly unlikely top boy but it soon became clear that his middle-class upbringing had enabled him to control a lucrative narcotics business.

Patrick grew up in a large, expensive semi-detached house right on the edge of one of east London's most notorious council estates. He later told me: "I was a walking contradiction. I went to public school yet my dad was a Caribbean who'd walked out on his family long ago. Meanwhile my mum held down a very important job while bringing me up as a single parent.

"But being a young kid with an absent father made me acceptable to many other kids on the local estate that was so near my home."

Patrick's mother had no idea that her intelligent, well-spoken teenage son was going to eventually train himself up to become a notorious top boy.

Patrick explained: "I had the best of both worlds, in a sense. I was a bit embarrassed to be going to a fee-paying school, so I told my mates on the estate it was a 'special school' because I had learning difficulties. I even changed my accent to sound more 'street'.

"My mum was working such long hours at her accountant's job in the City that she had no idea what I was up to."

But Patrick's middle-class life and his burgeoning secret career as a street gangster soon collided. He explained: "I went absent from school. I hinted to my mum I was taking a few drugs and getting up to mischief but she never found out I was already running my own 'business'."

That "business" was making Patrick £5,000 a week by the time he'd turned seventeen.

He explained: "I was a kind of one-off. I spoke all the right lingo but I was also more than capable of pronouncing my h's and sounding like a good middle-class kid when I had to."

Patrick – still in his teens – ran his cocaine, ecstasy and cannabis operation from an abandoned council flat on the housing estate less than a hundred yards from his mother's £1 million home.

"I could see my mum's house from one of the windows. But I was a world away when I was in that shitty flat running my empire."

Patrick guarded his real identity and background with great care in those early days. "Only a couple of my crew knew where I even came from. The rest of my 'yungers' didn't ask no questions and I didn't give them no clues, either."

But as Patrick's reputation spread, he became increasingly bold and open about his operation.

He explained: "I felt like I ran that estate. The feds seemed to keep well out of the way. But I was young and naïve back then. I thought I ruled the world. I didn't watch my back enough."

RAID

As so many street gangsters have told me, success in the drugs business always brings with it even more risks.

As Patrick explained: "The more customers, the more problems. People talk. Others gossip and in the end you can be sure your enemies will start circling."

By this time, Patrick was supplying mainly cocaine and cannabis to more than five hundred customers each week.

"If you lived on the estate you'd know what I was up to," he explained. "But I took the attitude that no one would dare grass me up."

But Patrick's reign soon came crashing down when a swat team of feds smashed his mother's front door down and swooped through the house at five one morning.

"My poor old mum got the shock of her life. Up until that point she had no idea what I was into. I felt very bad that she'd gotten dragged into it," he explained.

"She was so upset she refused to help me get bail after I'd been arrested and I ended up spending six months banged up in approved school 'cos I was so young."

Patrick's activities had only come to the notice of the feds after one of his street gang rivals saw him entering his mother's house close to the estate. He explained: "This guy was a snake who'd had his eye on my business for a long time.

"He'd been buying drugs off me just in order to see how I operated. He only told the feds so they'd run me off the estate. It's a dog-eat-dog world out there."

Patrick's six months in custody did little to deter him from the path he was on. He went on: "Prison was a challenge. Many gangsters inside were suspicious of me because I didn't fit all the usual stereotypes. Some even thought I was working for the feds.

"So I got a few beatings but as word got around about what I'd been up to in the outside world, I started to get some respect."

One specific incident cemented Patrick's reputation inside prison. He explained: "This blud came in who'd been running territory right next to mine back home. He came on all big and strong to me.

"I knew he was testing me out before his soldiers took over all my spots. I either kept out of his way – which would be seen as a climbdown – or I confronted him man to man."

Patrick then spent a week planning his reaction. "I knew I'd only have one chance. If I fucked it up, I'd be left with nothing and someone would try to finish me off inside before I even got out."

Patrick went on: "So I lured this blud into a corner of the yard and went for him. He never even saw it coming. A bunch of lads surrounded us, so the screws couldn't see anything and I beat the crap out of him.

"It was the first time I'd ever had to resort to violence. On the outside, others had done it for me. I was shocked how easily I smashed him to bits.

"That day marked a big change in my character. Up until then, I'd been playing at being a gangster. Now I was 100 per cent a gangster."

ON A ROLL

Patrick's trial was eventually thrown out on a technicality and he was soon back in business. "I knew the feds were watching me but the great thing about an estate is that you always know if the feds are sniffing around because everyone tells you."

Having been kicked out of his mother's house, Patrick set up home and business in an abandoned flat on the nearby estate. "There I was, living and running a drugs empire in a shit flat close to the posh house I'd been brought up in.

"My mum wouldn't speak to me because she now knew what I was doing. It was a hard time for her but it was better this way because I didn't want her to be raided by the feds again after what happened earlier.

"She didn't see it that way, of course. She hated that I'd ended up being a drug-dealing criminal. This was the life she wanted me to avoid more than anything else. That's why she'd worked so hard to afford that house and send me to a posh school."

For the following five years, Patrick ran his drugs empire from a number of once abandoned flats located on that same council housing estate and another nearby one.

He explained: "I was more ruthless after that spell inside. Being a so-called top boy is all about projection. You have to show you ain't scared of nothing or no one, then few people will ever try and take you on."

Patrick admitted: "I commissioned my boys to hurt rivals and people who didn't pay for their drugs. But you don't hurt people just for the sake of it. You do it as a last resort and a sign to others not to cross you."

Patrick's street life and the polite middle-class boy he'd once been were two separate entities. He explained: "I never talked to my mum. There were loads of times when we saw each other in the street and she'd start coming towards me and I'd turn away and avoid her.

"But I had to keep doing that so the feds and my enemies got the message that we had no emotional connection to each other. Many gangsters' family members are kidnapped and seriously hurt by their enemies.

"I wanted them to believe I was the nastiest motherfucker out there. That I didn't care about no one, not even my mum. I thought I was being clever, but I was also being an arsehole because I should have at least told my mother why I'd walked away from her.

"But I still thought the life of a gangster was better than anything else. My crew were more important to me than my real family. As long as I kept them happy, then that was all that mattered."

As the *Top Boy* TV series outlines so effectively, street gang violence primarily revolves around territory. As Patrick explained: "Other gangsters kept circling my territory thinking that one day they'd take it all over. I was running one of the most profitable food businesses in London and I knew I was attracting the wrong sort of attention."

And in the middle of all this were the feds. Patrick explained: "They hated my guts. They even tried to get at me by visiting my mum every few months, just to wind me up.

"Then the feds started pulling in some of my biggest rivals and told them they hadn't closed me down because I was feeding them info about my enemies. They made out I was a snake, which is the kiss of death in my world.

"The feds were trying to provoke a war. They didn't care if any of us got killed. They'd failed to bang us up and now they'd resorted to guerrilla tactics."

"They hoped we'd all implode. Rival gangs were following me and then informing the feds about my movements because they wanted me off the scene.

"I became very paranoid. I was like a typical coke head, even though I'd never taken any dubs in my life. I didn't know who I could trust any more. I even became convinced that my then girlfriend – the mother of my child – was either helping the police or my enemies. Everywhere we went there was always someone shadowing us.

"In my twisted mind I couldn't dump her in case that pushed her into helping my enemies, if she hadn't been doing that in the first place."

REALITY DAWNS

Patrick's drug empire started crumbling. He explained: "My girl went home to her family up north because we was fighting so much. I still didn't know if she was working for the other side or not.

"Then I got rid of two of my most experienced crew because I felt I couldn't trust them no more.

"Then some kid from the estate asked me for some work. He was about the same age I'd been when I first got in the game.

"That made me realise I had nothing concrete to show for all I'd been doing for so many years. This kid wanted to be me. Why the fuck would he want to do that? If he joined me then this could be the beginning of the end of his life. I held his future life in my hands.

"Sure, I had hundreds of thousands of p's hidden in stashes all round London. But my girl had gone. My family didn't speak to me and even the soldiers I'd been closest to had now either gone or died.

"I was all alone in a shitty flat on a council estate. None of it had been worthwhile. My mum had tried so hard to help me be someone but I'd turned my back on her. I should have known better."

Patrick refused to give the kid a job. But the same youth then went off and formed a posse and tried to take over Patrick's territory. A vicious war ensued, which marked the beginning of the end for Patrick.

A few weeks after our last meeting, Patrick was arrested. This time all the charges stuck and he ended up in prison for a long stretch. Patrick became a Muslim inside.

Some months later, a man knocked on the door of my London home. When I opened it, he said he had a message from Patrick that he would come after me if I ever repeated the details of our meetings with anyone. That's another reason why I've had to give him a different name here. It's not just about protecting the guilty.

So Patrick the top boy was very much alive and well. Despite seeking out religion in prison, it seemed likely he'd be back in business once he got out of prison.

LIVING FOR TODAY

When Patrick is eventually released, he'll discover that today's street gangsters are even younger and more cold-blooded than when he first arrived on the scene.

A lot of these characters insist that their first loyalty is to their gang "family" and they're prepared to die for "the cause".

But delving deeper into their backgrounds you often discover they have another motivation that sums up the two sides of the life of a typical young street gangster in London today.

I was introduced to Danimal by a recently retired top boy I'd met through some old-school London criminals I've known for more than twenty years.

Danimal was extremely shy and suspicious and immediately announced how proud he was of his gangster life, and insisted – like so many – that his crew meant much more to him than his family. Danimal greatly reminded me of the children selling drugs for Dris and Jaq on the corners of *Top Boy*'s fictional Summerhouse Estate.

Danimal – just turned seventeen – has clear aspirations to be a top boy one day. He explained: "This is my life. I don't want no job in Foot Locker smellin' people's feet. Out here I can be whatever I want to be. And a lot of people round here give me respect because they know I'm lookin' out for dem."

But Danimal's route to the gangster life is peppered with domestic problems. No father. Four sisters. Cramped living on the fifteenth floor of a tower block. He undoubtedly feels a "duty" to provide for his younger siblings in just the way Jamie does in series three of *Top Boy*.

Top Boy has been criticised by some for giving its most brutal gangsters "an excuse" to be criminals. But this is the reality. If you're a teenage boy on a typical sink estate you're going to have to help out your family with the p's.

Family members usually turn a blind eye because without that extra injection of cash they couldn't survive and pay the bills.

Danimal explained: "We don't become gangsters just to drive BMWs and wear some bling round our necks. Our families live in a poverty trap. Most bigtime top boys stash all their money away and drive round in ten-year-old Ford Fiestas and pay all their family's bills."

Meanwhile, young gangster Danimal rarely thinks about the future. "What's the point? Some blud could walk round the corner and shoot me in the head and I be dead before I reached the floor. Much better to live for today. I got cash. I make sure my sisters and mum are okay. It's all thanks to the gangster life."

And you can be certain that the cash which Danimal and many other street gangsters "earn" will not be finding its way to high street banks any time soon.

One of Danimal's crew members spread his cash around in various stashes in the countryside near to the estate where they live and operate. Then he was kidnapped by a rival gang.

Danimal explained: "They tortured him till he told them where those stashes were. Trouble was that he was so scared that he couldn't remember the exact places where two of those stashes were.

"So they took him out into the country to show them and he still couldn't find the right spots, so they killed him. That money is still out there somewhere to this day."

CRASH AND BURN

While top boys and their crews work round the clock on London's inner-city housing estates, the drugs they sell have to get to them in the first place. And that can involve these young gangsters stepping out of their "safety zones".

The outside world is rife with different types of dangers compared to what they're used to on a daily basis inside a housing estate.

I tracked down Lucky after hearing about his remarkable story on the east London estate I visited as part of my research for this book. He'd somehow survived, despite breaking many of the classic rules of the streets.

Lucky worked for a street crew on an estate run by one of east London's most notorious top boys.

"I got this name because I'm still alive!" he explained with good reason.

Only a few months earlier, Lucky had picked up a 10kg load of Colombian cocaine from the docks in Essex with another soldier called Pitbull.

"Everything went well," explained Lucky. "We packed the food under the floor in the back of a van and headed back to east London.

"Anyway, we was driving over a flyover at Canary Wharf [in London's Docklands area] when Pitbull starts clutching his chest. He's only just managing to steer the van. We're veering all over the place."

There was no hard shoulder on the dual carriageway as Pitbull struggled to stay conscious. Lucky grabbed the wheel and tried to slow it down so he could hop out and swap places with him.

"But then he slumped over the wheel," explained Lucky.

The van skidded out of control and over the edge of the flyover.

"Fortunately, we wasn't high up and I was strapped in. We landed on our side, but before I could scramble out, the feds were on the scene.

"They was real nice at first. Pitbull was out cold. Turns out he'd had a heart attack. When the feds asked for my ID, I said I didn't have it on me. I wasn't driving, so it was no big deal and the van was registered in Pitbull's name anyway.

"An ambulance turned up and the feds insisted I went to hospital to see how serious my injuries were. It was only then I realised Pitbull was dead.

"I freaked out and tried to get up and leave the scene. The feds shoved me back in the ambulance. They thought I was in shock and in a way I was."

Half a mile further down the road, Lucky managed to get out of the ambulance and made a run for it. The police never even knew his real name.

But Lucky's problems were only just beginning. He

explained: "I was in deep shit because if you lose the food for any reason it's down to you.

"I thought about runnin' but why bother? They'd find me and kill me anyway. My top boy was a mightily hard gangster. But I called him and told him the truth.

"He wasn't happy at all and said I had twenty-four hours to get the food back or they'd come and get me. At least the feds had no idea there was food still hidden in that smashed-up van."

Lucky needed to find the van and remove the drugs from it as quickly as possible. Meanwhile, the local police were suspicious about the van and had booked a technician to examine it properly the following day.

Lucky recalled: "At this stage, I still didn't even know where the van was. Then I remembered something. My top boy was so paranoid he always tracked us with his phone whenever we was driving a shipment from the docks."

Lucky went on: "Pitbull's phone had been on the dashboard when we crashed, so it had to be somewhere in the van. The phone's tracking device would tell me where it had been taken to."

Lucky and an associate found the police compound where the van was parked early the next morning. They climbed over a security fence, broke into the vehicle and pulled out the drugs.

"The feeling of relief was fuckin' overwhelming! I got it back to my boss. Then he told me he presumed I'd never get the drugs back.

"He said he wouldn't have topped me for losing the gear but I didn't believe him. I think he just said that to make sure I stayed loyal to him for other jobs we did after that."

ON THE FRONT LINE

The real street gang world is cruel and calculating. Gangs often put more importance on the brand of tracksuit they wear than the broken lives of the youths who join their ranks.

A typical London soldier tends to be between fifteen and nineteen, tall, slim and fit. Naturally, he'll most likely come from a broken family and he'll see his membership of a gang as a step up the ladder when it comes to being accepted by his peers.

I met P-Man through one of his mates, who'd helped me with a true crime documentary I made a few years back. Obviously, trust is not an easy thing to earn with these characters.

P-Man is sixteen. He has a No. 1 haircut and dresses in a designer T-shirt, tracksuit bottoms and trainers, rounded off by a gold chain round his neck. P-Man has spent much of the afternoon and early evening loitering by the ground floor entrance to a tower block in one of east London's most notorious concrete jungles.

When one of P-Man's four mobile phones rings, he answers fast and speaks in a low voice: "Six halves, bruv, yeah. No problem."

P-Man then snaps his eyes at his mates, nods slowly and says, 'Back soon, bluds', before sauntering off towards another corner of the estate.

Constantly checking out the area in front and behind him, P-Man ducks down a quiet alleyway that leads to one of the estate's garage areas, which consists of dozens of lock-ups and a small car park under the shadow of an enormous tower block.

A newish Volvo SUV rolls up just as P-Man stops in front of a rusting garage door. The driver is a middle-aged, middle-class-looking blonde woman. The electric window buzzes down. A manicured hand passes crisp £20 bank notes in the direction of a vaguely smiling P-Man. He hands over a see-through zippy bag containing six small wraps and smiles.

"Ya good," says P-Man, as the window goes back up and the Volvo slides off.

These are the real young street gangsters on the front line. This type of scene is repeated across London's inner-city council estates probably thousands of times every day of the week.

A few minutes later, P-Man and I sat down for a coffee in one of the trendy cafes that has sprung up around this area of east London, in recent years.

As we chatted, P-Man's phone went again. He ignored it. "Dey can wait. Dubs junkies de worst. Always expectin' ya to drop everytin' and run ta dem."

P-Man never refers to his produce as "drugs". It's either food or more specific terms like dubs for cocaine and crack and B for brown, which is heroin.

P-Man and his fellow soldiers tread very carefully in case the feds and their enemies are on the lookout for them. One of P-Man's crew members was recently arrested by the police and forced by detectives to agree to give evidence against his gang. P-Man explained: "They told him they'd get his family evicted from their flat on an estate unless he helped them. That's tough to handle, so he went over the other side."

The feds gave their new gang informant immunity from prosecution and agreed for his family to join him in protective custody in a house in the north of England. P-Man explained: "We been searching for him ever since we heard but no one knows exactly where he is. Once we find out, then he's gonna be dead meat."

The phone rings three more times before P-Man finally answers it with a cool, "Whatsup bruv?" Seconds later my meeting with P-Man is over and he's on his way to another drugs transaction.

RAT LINE

It's not surprising that paranoia rules many street gangs. And if anyone is suspected of being an informant it can wreck the unity of an entire crew.

In *Top Boy* series one, "younger" Gem is pressurised by the feds to provide them with evidence that bosses Dushane and Sully murdered a drugs rival.

In real life, anyone on an estate who is even remotely suspected of being a "rat" has to watch his or her back, even if they're just kids. For breaking this golden rule often sparks murder and mayhem.

Early in 2020, I met a street gang soldier called Jinx whose real-life story is more chilling than the plotline from any episode of *Top Boy*. It wasn't easy coaxing him out to be interviewed, for reasons I will explain later.

Jinx first worked for a gang on his estate as a spotter aged twelve and then as a soldier when he turned fourteen. His top boy even paid him to shadow a rival drug dealer and report his movements back to him.

Jinx obeyed orders but then that rival drug dealer was shot dead, thanks to the information Jinx had provided to his top boy. It was a massive wake-up call for the teenager.

He explained: "I saw this blud's body in the playground on our estate. They'd laid it out on a kids' roundabout. It completely did my head in.

"Suddenly, I got shit-scared of everything I was involved in. I feared that one day that could be me on that roundabout."

For some months Jinx didn't breath a word to anyone about his role in that drug dealer's murder.

He explained: "I kept to the code. My top boy knew I was nervous after the murder and he kept a close eye on me. But he didn't have to warn me not to speak. I just knew the rules."

Then Jinx was picked up by the feds after being spotted by officers selling drugs on the estate.

He explained: "They tried to get me to talk about my top boy and the whole crew and then asked me about the murder. I said nothing at first like I'd always been told to."

Jinx's top boy even paid for a lawyer to represent Jinx while he was being interrogated by police.

He went on: "This brief [lawyer] reminded me not to talk about anything to do with the murder. Basically he was passing on a threat from my top boy."

However, unknown to Jinx the police had found CCTV footage clearly showing him shadowing the same drug dealer just before he was murdered.

Jinx explained: "The feds said I'd be charged with murder, even though I didn't do it. I didn't know what to do. I had nowhere to turn. I thought I'd be going to jail, if I didn't help them."

But Jinx's lawyer insisted that the CCTV proved nothing except that Jinx had walked past the murdered drug dealer shortly before he was killed. He was eventually released without charge.

But this left Jinx in an even bigger dilemma. He explained: "I couldn't walk away from my top boy, otherwise he'd think I'd helped the feds in some way. I was fucked.

"I had no choice but to carry on working on the estate. I hated every minute of it from that moment on and I felt bad each time I passed that dead drug blud's family on the estate. I even seriously thought about killing myself."

Less than a year later, Jinx's top boy got sent to jail after another gang member informed on him.

Jinx added: "That was my chance to get out. I left the estate immediately and never went back there ever again.

"I heard that my crew thought about getting one of the yungers to top me. But it never happened."

SENDING OUT A MESSAGE

Fear and trepidation undoubtedly help today's street gangs to exert power and influence within their community. Some crews even have their own in-house "specialists" to keep the troops in line and to "deal" with troublesome outsiders.

Hitting your enemies first is a prerequisite in this world. There is no time to reconsider options, which means killings and beatings rarely get cancelled once they've been commissioned.

That's where Fem comes in. I'd heard about her for a couple of years through one of my neighbours, who lived near me on a notorious west London housing estate. She was said to be one of the few hitwomen to have ever worked for a street gang. What I went on to hear about Fem reminded me a great deal of *Top Boy* character Jaq, although Fem sounded even more detached.

I wasn't able to talk directly to Fem but I did manage to contact two former members of her crew who revealed her inside story, which is so chilling that I had to feature it in this book.

Today Fem is twenty three years old but she started in the food game on the estate at the age of just fifteen.

One of her former associates told me: "Fem's a freak. She's a girl but she don't act like one. She hates most bluds for a start. Mind you that probably helps her kill 'em more easily."

The key to Fem's job as a professional killer is her ability as a woman to avoid the long arm of the feds.

Fem's fellow gang member went on: "Being a girl helps her stay under the radar. The other thing is that none of us know much about her personal life. She could be gay like that Jaq on *Top Boy* but no one's ever dared ask her cos she's a scary piece of work."

Other gang members told how Fem became her crew's in-house hit lady after urging her then top boy to kill one of their street dealers suspected of being a police informant.

"Fem just wouldn't leave it alone," explained one gang member. "She told her top boy this blud had to die. The rest of us were not so sure he was even a rat and urged our top boy to hold back and establish the true facts first. But then Fem just went and shot the dude in cold blood in front of most of us.

"At first we was very angry. But then Fem produced evidence which proved beyond doubt that this blud had been a rat and from that moment on she became our top killer."

And Fem worked to a very specific set of rules.

The same former gang member explained: "She wouldn't kill women or kids and we respected her for that. But she had this way of looking at us bluds like she hated us, even when she was smiling and gettin' high. We was dirt to her."

Details of Fem's other alleged victims are hard to come by as street crew members don't like admitting anything that might be later used as evidence to put them in jail.

But one former gang member added: "Fem knows that every time she kills a blud, it sends out a message to all our enemies. She even leaves her victims in places where everyone can see them. That scares the shit out of everyone and stops anyone from talking to the feds."

None of the street gangsters would reveal anything about Fem's real identity. She didn't come from the gang's own home estate and no one was prepared to even admit they knew her real name.

"She'd come after anyone she thought was talkin' about her," said one crew member.

It's important to point out here that some female gang members face regular abuse at the hands of their male counterparts and are exploited for sex along with female relatives of gang members.

TRAINED TO KILL

There are some even more deadly gang members than Fem out there. A handful of the older ones come from a services background, which means they've already been trained as professional killers before they even join a street crew.

These characters are very different from the young men who make up the majority of gangs. They've come into the "business" late after leaving the services and finding no opportunities in the real outside world.

I managed to track down one such gangster called Dogface through one of his one-time army commanding officers, who'd stayed in touch with him despite the fact he was working for a London street gang.

My source told me that Dogface was like a walking tinder-box about to blow up at any moment and warned me to watch my back because he had a short temper and was prone to bouts of violence.

Dogface had been jobless and drifting for more than two years without any real direction after quitting the army following three active tours of duty in Iraq and Afghanistan. He eventually ended up back on the same housing estate in west London where he'd grown up.

He explained: "I'd gone full circle. My head was all over the place because of everything I'd been through in the army and now I was on my own and lost in the real world. It was not a good place to be in.

"Trouble is when I came back I was a different person. The army just doesn't prepare you for the 'come down'. I quickly spiralled into depression and hopelessness. I needed money and excitement in that order."

Dogface was still in his twenties and had continued to stay fit, despite leaving the army. He explained: "I'd presumed I'd get a job in private security and earn some decent money but it never happened."

Whilst Dogface had been away on the killing fields of Iraq and Afghanistan, his home estate had turned from a barren, rundown community into a gang-dominated neighbourhood where most law- abiding citizens feared to tread, especially after dark.

Dogface explained: "It was virtually a war zone not unlike where I'd just come back from. I couldn't understand how it had ended up that way."

But then an incident occurred on the estate that changed Dogface's life. He explained: "These two kids of about fifteen jumped me when I was on a walkway on the estate. They had no idea who I was and I beat the crap out of them."

It soon emerged that his attackers sold "food" for the estate's top boy. Dogface explained: "I found all this out when this top boy and three of his crew turned up at my mum's front door.

"They'd no doubt come to punish me for smashing those two kids up. The top boy was even armed with a gun, which he flashed at me as I opened the door.

"But I'd seen more guns than hot dinners during my tours of duty, so a few kid gangsters trying to put pressure on me didn't mean a thing.

"I told the top boy that I could easily take 'em down – guns or no guns – and it would make more sense for me to earn some money by working for him.

"I'd never intended to work in the food game. But I'd looked at their bling and thought, 'What the fuck. I may as well have a crack at this. What have I got to lose? Fuck all.'

"And then there was the buzz. In the army this was constant and I greatly missed that feeling of excitement and fear."

Dogface's first fully fledged "assignment" involved hiding a shipment of cocaine in the floor of a Ford Transit van that he was then going to deliver to a house "out in the country".

That first job netted Dogface two thousand much needed pounds. "I was in. I'd been accepted by the top boy and his crew. I think they looked on me as their security blanket and a bit of a father figure. As long as I was around, they believed that no one would fuck with them."

Dogface was then encouraged by his top boy to be the middleman between them and the Eastern European gangsters who were supplying shipments of cocaine to the estate crew at that time.

"These foreign gangsters gave me massive respect because of my services background. They wanted me to be the top boy on the estate. But I made sure the real top boy didn't find that out."

Within a month, Dogface had agreed to drive to France to pick up a shipment of cocaine. "But this time it was a much bigger amount," he explained. "That first pick-up had been a test by the top boy. This time I was being put to work properly but all I cared about was that they mentioned a £10,000 fee this time."

Dogface explained: "The adrenaline rush when I got back to the estate with the food after that pick-up was extraordinary. It looked as if everything had gone smoothly and now all we needed to do was make sure all the food was safely unpacked and I'd get my £10,000."

But then things started to go wrong. Dogface explained: "The top boy told me that the guys I'd made the pick-up from in France had called him to say they thought I'd acted very suspiciously and that I should be searched for wires to make sure I wasn't working for the feds.

"I was outraged by these accusations and had a big row with the top boy. In the end, I had to be dragged off him by two of his soldiers. I was lucky they didn't shoot me or stab me there and then."

For the following two weeks, Dogface was ordered not to leave his flat on the estate until the top boy and his soldiers had checked out he wasn't a "spy". He explained: "In the end, I passed all the checks and the top boy apologised. I think he realised his mistake and didn't want to lose me.

"But then I heard one of his soldiers had put around the original rumour that I was a rat because he'd been jealous of the way the top boy had promoted me to his number two over the head of this guy."

Dogface saved all the money he earned working for the gang and moved off the estate after his mother died.

"Surprisingly, no one came after me. Maybe they decided I wasn't worth the trouble. But I was definitely one of the lucky ones because you don't normally get to walk away that easily."

DOSE OF REALITY

Dogface was one of the lucky ones. It's rare for street gangs to allow their crew members to simply walk away without reprisals. Yet it's surprising how many youngsters with aspirations to be in a street crew have no idea about that golden rule.

That's why many of the gangsters I've spoken to believe that *Top Boy*'s gritty portrayal of London's urban drug gangs could actually help make the capital's streets safer in the long term.

Former crew member Daz explained: "*Top Boy* is a dose of reality for any kid who thinks selling drugs is gonna be the answer to his problems. You see what happens to people that shoot other people. They don't live happily ever after. They often end up dead in a ditch."

Daz was a member of a street gang on a west London housing estate. He explained: "I ticked all the right boxes for getting caught up in a crew. No dad. Mum was sick. The crew provided me with support when I needed it most.

"I didn't question their motives, even when they started using me at just thirteen to carry drugs around the estate in case their rivals or the feds tried to get hold of it.

"It was dangerous work for a kid barely in his teens. And when they told me to carry a blade with me at all times 'just in case', I just did what I was told.

"After all, they'd cared for me when no one else had. How could I be disloyal after that?"

Daz was so disengaged from the so-called normal world that when he heard about another young gangster being killed in the street it meant nothing to him.

He explained: "I just presumed he deserved it cos he'd come onto our territory. That was how it worked and he should have known better. I never once thought about his mum, his sisters or his brothers. I didn't have that kind of support, so why should I care about someone else's family?"

Then Daz was ordered by his top boy to carry a shipment of drugs to another town outside London. He explained: "My top boy was called Hit for good reason. He scared the shit out of me. I had to go on a train out into the countryside with a holdall full of coke and weed.

"But another kid in the gang had been nicked the previous week doing exactly the same thing, so I said I wasn't happy. What a mistake that was.

"Hit went crazy at me and told me I had no choice. Then he smashed me in the face with these knuckledusters. I was bleeding everywhere and then he kicked me as I lay curled up on the floor.

"I was terrified. Suddenly the gang was no longer my family. They were my enemy and Hit was the devil in charge of them."

Daz was advised by two other crew members to clean himself up and pick up the drugs, otherwise Hit would finish him off.

Daz recalled: "It felt like my family had rejected me because Hit was still so angry with me. It was the loneliest feeling I've ever had.

"I had no one to turn to. I knew if I didn't go back and get the food, Hit and his soldiers would come after me and destroy me.

"But I also knew that if I got caught like my mate the previous week then I'd most likely end up in jail.

"I hated Hit with a vengeance for being such a bully towards me."

Daz then called Hit on his mobile and told him he'd carry the food after all. But Daz's nose had been broken during Hit's assault on him so he needed to go to hospital first to get it fixed before taking the drugs out of town.

Daz explained: "He sounded right pissed off with me but agreed to meet me in the hospital car park after I'd been treated."

Top boy Hit parked his BMW up in front of the hospital at least an hour early as a reminder to Daz that he was waiting for him.

Minutes later, Daz watched from the hospital waiting room as armed feds surrounded Hit's car and arrested him for carrying a gun plus that holdall full of drugs, which he'd been planning to force Daz to transport.

He recalled: "I was stunned and terrified I'd be accused by him and the crew of alerting the feds."

But word soon spread on Daz's estate that Hit had been picked up after his stolen car registration number was spotted by the hospital's CCTV. Even to this day, Daz refuses to say if he informed the police about the drugs shipment.

Daz explained: "Hit went to prison for a long time and none of his soldiers ever came near me in revenge. I reckon most of them were as relieved as me that he was behind bars."

Today, Daz has a partner and two children and works as a gang co-ordinator dealing with many teenagers who're like he once was. "I don't preach to any of them. I just tell it like it is.

"That's why shows like *Top Boy* are so important for kids. They can see there is no glamour in being a drug dealer. Everything's run on fear. You never know what's lying in wait around the corner. That's no way to lead your life."

BREAKING THE RULES

Top Boy's dramatic storylines are often reflected in real life when it comes to the so-called gangster code of the street. For revenge drives many aspects of London's street crew world.

That can even mean gangs hunting down and killing their enemies when they all live on the same housing estate.

These estates are self-contained communities in many ways. As one young gangster told me: "What goes in an estate doesn't always come out and that includes people who've crossed gangs. They are secretive places and the people in them know to live by a certain code."

No wonder the police are rarely alerted to any law breakers. As the same young gangster explained: "You can't call in the feds and see if they'll grab the bad guys for you because you're most likely a bad guy yourself."

In 2019, I heard about a young street gangster called Tinks who broke all these so-called "rules".

Tinks had been the bag man for a crew selling drugs on one of south London's biggest housing estates. That meant he had to carry large sums of cash around to ensure that no one apart from the gang's top boy knew where all this money was at any one time.

One of Tinks's fellow soldiers later explained: "This was a high-risk job and Tinks got well paid for it. But none of us would want to do what he had to do.

"Everyone's after you. Other crews want to find you, so they can steal your cash. Your own crew will always blame you if any of those p's go missing. It's a no-win job with a short life expectancy."

But Tinks liked it because it was edgy and made him feel important. His crew all looked up to him and admired him for taking so many risks. But danger was constantly lurking around every corner.

Tinks's old associate continued: "One time, Tinks was sent to make a payment to the suppliers for a dubs shipment. Something happened and he came back with no cash and no dubs."

Tinks insisted to his top boy that the suppliers had taken the cash from him and refused to give him the drugs at gunpoint when they met.

But the suppliers claimed they handed Tinks the drugs and he'd run off without giving them their cash. No one knew who to believe but someone was going to have to pay for it.

The same crew member went on: "The suppliers got very heavy about it. They told us we had twenty-four hours to pay the cash and find the dubs or they'd start culling us, and they meant it."

Meanwhile, Tinks still insisted he'd given the money to the suppliers and they'd gone off without giving him the drugs. His top boy was inclined to believe him.

Then the feds turned up on the estate and said they knew what had happened and offered the crew immunity from prosecution if they gave evidence against the suppliers.

Tinks smelt a rat. He and his crew even wondered if the police had deliberately stolen the drugs from the suppliers in order to start a gang war, which would then result in heavy losses on both sides.

The same soldier went on: "The feds were capable of that. But we'd never snitch on anyone, not even those psycho bunnies suppliers, so we told the feds where to go."

However, the top boy and his crew knew they had to do something before a war broke out. They still believed Tinks but made it clear he had to come up with a plan to force the suppliers to retreat.

The soldier continued: "Then Tinks offers to disappear and we'd tell the suppliers we killed him."

But some crew members suspected that Tinks had stolen the money and the drugs himself and was planning to disappear with everything anyway. Those crew members insisted Tinks should pay the ultimate price.

Tinks knew his life was hanging in the balance. Then he had a lucky break. He found out there were three CCTV cameras overlooking the car park where the alleged transaction had taken place with the suppliers.

Tinks's gang associate explained: "Tinks brought us footage that showed him handing the actual holdall containing the cash over to the suppliers as they stood next to his car. Now we knew they were conning us."

But this presented Tinks' street gang with another problem. They didn't want to challenge the suppliers because they were their main dubs suppliers. It was vital they kept them happy or else their food would dry up.

Tinks was immediately ordered to leave London and never come back. The suppliers were told Tinks was dead. They were suspicious at first but eventually accepted the story and the debt was wiped clean and they continue doing business with each other.

Tinks is said to have moved abroad and has never been seen again. No one to this day knows if he is alive or dead.

Some are convinced Tinks was *iced* after all. One local gang member explained: "We reckon his own top boy had it done to save face."

OUT OF CONTROL

Killings are often carried out within street gangs as a warning to members not to be tempted to work for other crews or talk to the police.

But gang members can also find themselves at the centre of this type of internal threat because of something relatively unimportant.

Street gangster Fizz is a classic example. He explained: "My experience sums it all up. One time I was wearing a brand new pair of £200 trainers and this other blud in the same crew reckoned they belonged to him.

"This fam then went to the top boy and said I'd broken into his place and stolen them trainers. No one believed him but he got angrier and angrier and – in the end – came after me."

"I was on a walkway between two blocks of flats on the estate when he and two of his bluds jumped me. They gave me a good kicking, pulled the trainers off my feet and called me a pussy.

"I was mad as hell. I wanted to shoot that bastard for what he'd done. I got together my crew and we went looking for him."

As he searched the estate, Fizz bumped into his own girl-friend and told her what had happened. Instead of urging him to seek retribution, she calmed him down.

Fizz explained: "She said them trainers weren't important. I was just trying to save face in front of the rest of my crew."

At first, Fizz ignored his girlfriend's pleas and continued his plan to hit back at the other crew member. Then Fizz was reminded by her that the other gangster had only taken the trainers because he liked the look of them.

"My girl said that was a pathetic reason to kill someone and she was right. I was about to risk my life over some fuckin' trainers. She said it was a warning from God to get out of the crew before it was too late. So I walked away from it all."

Fizz was fortunate enough to have a girlfriend who helped him turn his attitude around. They both eventually moved off the estate and he turned his back on the gangster life.

STREET SMART

The eclectic mix of residents on today's London housing estates means that street gangsters themselves can come from a wide variety of backgrounds and countries.

One such character called Prince summed it up when he told me: "You get all sorts in estates like mine and some decide to escape them while others find themselves trapped on them."

I tracked down Prince through a 'Ghanaian-based underworld contact who worked in the cocaine business more than twenty years ago. Prince was the most relaxed street gangster I've ever met. He acted as if he didn't have a care in the world.

Prince's Ghanaian father abandoned him and his mother on a west London housing estate before he was even born a quarter of a century ago. Prince explained: "My mother got pregnant by this rich Ghanaian guy and I was the result. But his family didn't want nothing to do with us, so he went back to Ghana and left us here."

Prince grew up on the breadline. Like so many young males on housing estates in London, he joined a street gang as soon as he reached his teens. He recalled: "I had no choice. My mum was sick. I had to keep finding money to look after her."

Not surprisingly, the local top boy became like a father figure to Prince. He explained: "For the first time in my life I had someone to look up to and respect. I was a quick learner and by the time I was seventeen I was the top boy handling food for the entire estate.

"But I didn't much like the old-school white guys I was buying the food from. They was nasty, racist bastards and treated us all like shit because they knew we had to have their product.

"Often they'd rip us off by selling us over-cut food but we couldn't do nothing about it because we couldn't get food from no place else.

"Then those bastards doubled the price of the food and told us they'd kill us if we complained, and we all believed them cos they was such hard nuts."

After more than a year buying shipments from the old-school Brits, Prince decided he'd had enough. "I got my best mate to take over all the food on the estate and I headed off to Ghana. I wanted to find my father and my mum wanted to go home."

In the 'Ghanaian capital of Accra, Prince found himself ostracised because his father refused to see him and threatened to have him and his mother killed if they didn't leave the country.

"It was shit out there," explained Prince. "My poor old mum was very sick. All she wanted was to stay in Ghana and die surrounded by her family.

"Instead we was given a week to get out and if we didn't, I'd be locked up for drug dealing. My dad had many friends in the police in Accra and he was so ashamed of me he was prepared to do this in order to get me out of his life."

Prince contacted his old crew back on his estate in London to see if he could get some work on his return to the UK capital.

"They was in pieces," explained Prince. "The old-school Brits were charging them so much for food that the profits were tumbling fast.

"There was clearly no point in going back to London. My mum needed proper healthcare. I didn't know which way to turn."

Prince then met a man in Accra who was from the nearby West African country of Guinea-Bissau. "He told me GB was a narco state, man. The Colombians had started using it as a transport hub for all the cocaine they smuggled into the UK and Europe from South America."

In fact, the Colombian cartels ran Guinea-Bissau. They paid for everything: the schools, the hospitals, and in exchange they were allowed to bring all their cocaine through this tiny nation and then ship it up through Africa and across the Mediterranean to Europe and Britain.

Prince explained: "I decided I was going to buy food direct from the Colombians in Guinea-Bissau. My mates back in London thought I was crazy when I first told them but what did I have to lose?"

So Prince and his sick mum moved to Bissau, the capital of Guinea-Bissau. "I couldn't even get near the Colombians at first. The locals were all trained to deny the Colombians even existed there. You can't just ring them up. You have to go through a local contact, who usually turns out to be a crooked fed."

Prince continued: "And the locals in Bissau didn't like 'Ghanaians either. In the end I started pretending to be a local myself."

Two months after first arriving in Bissau, Prince finally secured a meeting with one of the Colombian cartel "managers" residing in the capital city.

"They checked me out real good. They even went back to people who knew me in London to make sure I was genuine. At one stage I thought they'd shoot me because a lot of the locals thought I was a DEA spy."

But within weeks of that first meeting, Prince secured a deal with the Colombians to buy their product in Guinea-Bissau and then pay his own transport costs to get the drugs to London.

Prince explained: "They was very clever. They gave me the food on credit at first and even provided the transport links. That way they knew I couldn't change my mind and walk away from the deal and I was a dead man if I didn't pay them back. But I never had any plans to do a runner."

Prince then set everything up with his crew back in London. They even worked out how to make sure all the drugs were safely picked up when they arrived by ship at Tilbury Docks just down the Thames from his old estate.

Prince explained: "But then the Colombians came back and said the deal was off because the old-school Brits had heard about my plan and they wanted to stop it at all costs. They didn't want the street gangs back in the UK getting ideas about buying direct from the Colombians, for obvious reasons."

Shortly after this Prince was arrested by police in Guinea-Bissau, who said he was in the country illegally. He explained: "I didn't know if the Colombians wanted me out or whether the locals had been pressurised by the old-school Brits."

After two days in a stinking cell, Prince was released from jail in Bissau. At the prison gate, he was met by a delegation of Colombians.

"I was shittin' myself when I saw them," Prince later explained. "They made me get in their van and I thought that was it. The deal had collapsed and now they was making sure I didn't blabber and my life was over."

In fact, the Colombians got Prince to call his crew back in London to find out if they were prepared to take on the old-school Brits.

Prince explained: "So I got on the phone and pretended to talk to my man. I told him to fuck the Brits because if we won we'd make a fortune by getting our food direct from the Colombians.

"The Colombians were very impressed. Then I made another fake call to London to arrange for one of the Brits to be iced to send a message to them that we would be bringing in our own supplies of food from now on."

For the next forty-eight hours, Prince waited for the Colombians to come back and confirm the cocaine deal was back on. "If they pulled out, I knew I was a dead man.

"Then out of the blue I get a call from my man in London. The old-school Brits had been in touch. I took a breath. This had to be bad news. I even wondered if the Brits were there pointing a gun at my blud's head as he spoke to me.

"But my blud said the Brits had given us permission to buy our food direct from the Colombians in Guinea-Bissau. I was stunned. Why would they go and do that?

"It turned out that the Colombians had pressurised the Brits to make an exception for me. The main guy in Guinea-Bissau had taken a shine to me and they wanted to explore alternative arrangements because they felt the Brits were on the verge of being pushed out of the UK.

"It just shows how powerful the Colombians are. The Brits were given no choice and of course they didn't want to risk losing any of their shipments from South America."

However, there was one condition. Prince's crew back in London were not allowed to admit to any other gangs that they were getting their cocaine direct from the Colombians in Guinea-Bissau.

Prince explained: "This was done to keep the Brits quiet but also because the Colombians didn't want any other strange faces turning up in Bissau asking questions."

Today, Prince and his sickly mother remain in Guinea-Bissau. He describes himself as a businessman and keeps a very low profile, and they live in a smart penthouse apartment in the capital.

Prince explained: "I'm happy here. No one will touch me as long as I stay on side with the Colombians.

"I've got a nice home. My mum is being properly cared for. Sure, I miss my bluds back in London but I'm leading a better life than I could ever have dreamed of.

"The Colombians are good to deal with as long as you don't cross them. They control the government here, so if I have any problems with the police they step in and sort it all out. That doesn't happen in London or Ghana.

"Sometimes I think it's all gonna blow up in my face one day. But why should it? Sure, the Colombians are running a drug empire, but the money they pump into this country has saved it from the scrap heap. Is that really such a bad thing?

THE GATEKEEPER

Back in London, Colombian drug cartels keep a much lower profile although their priority remains to ensure their best customers are "fed" product at all times of the day and night.

This means a complex web of front companies and "representatives" occupying a shadowy role inside the UK capital's drugs underworld.

Today, the Colombians even go out of their way to employ people who are not from Latin America, so that they more easily slip below the London police radar.

In December 2019, I was introduced to South African-born Tic-Toc by a Colombian woman who's been working for a cartel for more than thirty years.

Tic-Toc is a fascinating link man between the coke smuggling hubs that thrive in his home country and elsewhere on the African continent.

The South American cartels have deliberately targeted developing nations to smuggle their cocaine through, as is perfectly illustrated through the experiences of top boy Prince in Guinea-Bissau.

In December 2019, I accompanied Tic-Toc on a visit inside the middle of an area controlled by one of south London's most notorious street gangs. I entered a warehouse on an industrial estate just south of the River Thames with Tic-Toc, whom I had originally contacted through another source of mine from back when I lived in southern Spain ten years ago.

Tic-Toc is protected by two burly "associates" and his identity is hidden by sunglasses. He is wearing a natty dark brown three-piece suit and definitely does not look like a typical street gangster.

"Great place, yeah?" says Tic-Toc with a glint of sunlight bouncing off his shades. "We pay all the right people, so no one gives us no trouble."

Tic-Toc says he's twenty-two but he seems younger. He claims he's been working in "the supply business" since he was thirteen.

However, today Tic-Toc is the Colombians' *gatekeeper* in south London. As he talks, his "team" clinically break up one kilo packs of cocaine into smaller plastic vacuum containers, which will then be delivered to the drug suppliers, who in turn feed most of the street gangs.

The Colombians trust operatives like Tic-Toc to handle their cocaine once it arrives in London, so they can claim a bigger chunk of the profits. One old drug smuggling vet told me that the South Americans have a ten-year plan for London. "They've come back into this end of the business because their profit margins are falling."

Tic-Toc insists he's never even come close to being arrested, despite spending much of the last five years handling coke on virtually a daily basis.

Meanwhile, other street gangsters appear blindly fearless and prepared to turn the streets of London into their own killing fields.

NEVER STOOD A CHANCE

BRIXTON, SOUTH LONDON: FEBRUARY 2019

No one took much notice of the Black BMW with darkened windows that pulled up outside the Marcus Lipton Youth Centre, a place where teenagers socialised in safety away from nearby housing estates.

Moments later, two youths jumped out of the BMW. They were armed with long knives and ran at speed towards a group of teenagers gathered near the youth club entrance, who then darted inside the main building.

One of those attackers from the BMW was R1, a notorious top boy with a fearsome reputation.

"Everything happened really fast... The boys came running through the hall that we were working in. Everyone was really alarmed," one witness later recalled.

One of the young men being chased – twenty-three-year-old Glendon Spence – fell over and was cornered by R1 and his accomplice near a table tennis table. He was stabbed in his hand and arm as he fought to fend off the attackers. Then one blade punctured Spence's thigh, penetrating a major artery. He fell to the floor and his assailants turned and ran out back towards their car.

Victim Spence managed to struggle to his feet, before collapsing in a heap on the floor once again as people gathered around him. Despite the efforts of club members and paramedics, Spence died on the floor of the youth club he'd attended since childhood.

The BMW used by Spence's killers was found burnt out and abandoned less than an hour later on the edge of a nearby housing estate. Glendon Spence's murder was just one of a hundred violent killings in London which occurred in the first four months of 2019.

The feds probing the Spence killing soon hit an early obstacle. Key witnesses refused to talk to them, so they couldn't even establish if the attack had been gang related.

Then detectives had a surprising breakthrough. During the attack, a youth worker at the club overheard one of the attackers call his accomplice "R1". The fed's gang intelligence officers soon worked out this was the street name for Rishon Florant, then aged seventeen, who had links to a south London gang and a string of convictions for knife possession.

R1 had been excluded from school and banned from entering the borough of Lambeth – where Brixton is located – at the time of the murder.

R1's name and description was immediately circulated to police and border officials at ports across the country. He was arrested at London's Heathrow Airport about to board a flight to Uganda. Fingerprints and CCTV helped to confirm his identity.

Back in Brixton, police were still hunting the missing second suspect. Then investigators sifting through footage from CCTV cameras located near the youth club noticed that one of the attackers had touched an outside gate and the table tennis table next to where Spence had been stabbed.

Forensic experts then recovered a clear fingerprint from both locations. On the national DNA database, they found a match to Chibuzo Ukonu, another seventeen-year-old youth with a criminal record for knife possession and drug dealing.

He was tracked to Manchester where he was arrested. Ukonu and R1 Florant eventually stood trial at London's Old Bailey.

R1 was convicted of murder and jailed for a minimum of eighteen years. As he walked from the dock to the cell, he smiled at his friends in the public galley when they shouted "Free R1". He has since lodged an appeal against his conviction.

Ukonu was found guilty of manslaughter and sentenced to fourteen years in a young offender institution.

Other youths who'd been involved in the build-up to the attack on Glendon Spence were never brought to justice.

THE NEW BOSSES

In the first series of *Top Boy*, set in 2011, old-school crime boss Bobby Raikes (played by Geoff Bell) pushes shipments of drugs to Summerhouse Estate gang boss Dushane, who admits to his trigger-happy partner Sully that they have to keep Bobby happy because he's their main supplier. Then Albanian gangsters begin appearing on the horizon and death and destruction soon follow.

Albania's own emergence as a "narco state" first began in 1990, following the collapse of the old Communist regime. More than 80,000 Albanian criminals turned up in Italy within months. Those gangsters soon spread west across Italy and the rest of Europe. Originally, they were the street dealers and the enforcers, but they were fast learners.

The Albanian Mafia even imported hash-growing experts from other countries to help introduce the crop to Albania. Today, about one-third of the hash supplied throughout Europe is grown in Albania.

Following the UK riots back in 2011, Albanian mobsters had initially watched from a distance as the Yardies and their street gangs disintegrated. By this time they were supplying drugs all over Western Europe and had even formed close connections to Colombian cartels and other South American drug suppliers.

By the end of 2011, gangs of trigger-happy Albanian criminals had moved into many of London's prime drug supply networks once held by the Yardies. The Albanians had round-the-clock access to arms and made sure the London underworld knew that they wouldn't hesitate to kill anyone who crossed them.

They even deliberately recruited youths from housing estates to sell their drugs on the streets because they knew many of the best customers could be inherited from the previous street gang operations. These Balkan gangs knew only too well how important it was that their street dealers came from the very same estates they were now selling drugs to. This uneasy connection between the Albanians and street gangs on London's housing estates went on to contribute even further to the city's ever-increasing knife epidemic.

The Albanians' fierce reputation for murdering anyone who crossed them meant that young street gangsters attacked rivals with impunity because they were terrified of losing territory to rival crews in case their Albanian bosses punished them.

Today a lot of top boy street crews inside London's housing estates try to minimise their contact with the Albanians but that is hard to do because these Balkan villains supply more than 80 per cent of the food shipments coming into the UK capital today.

The Albanians have been expertly undercutting the price of all rival drug shipments to the street gangs. They believe they "own" the right to run the London drugs underworld and they enforce that power by threatening to shoot anyone who defies them.

One former top boy explained: "You gotta remember, the Albanians quickly recruited the street gangs to distribute their product."

Street gangs similar to those portrayed in *Top Boy* found themselves with no choice but to buy their "food" from the Eastern Europeans. It's evolved into a marriage made in hell.

One former soldier recalled: "I remember the first time the Albanians tracked us down and told us they wanted us to buy their food. At first we was like, 'What the fuck?' They were evil-looking motherfuckers, even though they was all charming at first because they wanted us to keep selling their shit."

During my research into this book, I uncovered clear evidence that the Albanians killed a couple of old-school British gangsters when they first took over London's drug markets just to make an example of them.

"They hit us hard and ruthlessly," explained one retired London criminal. "It's a game to them and they don't want anyone standing in their way."

The killing of those two British gangsters also left the street gangs with no one else to purchase their food from.

As a result, today's London underworld works to a completely different set of rules when it comes to drugs.

FEAR

One former street gangster explained: "Any street crews who stood up to the Albanians tended to disappear.

"We've had no choice but to deal with those motherfuckers or we get fucked. And at the same time, the feds are all over us. The Albanians even said they'd grass us up to the feds if we don't play the game their way."

One former Scotland Yard drugs squad officer explained: "It's a tinderbox out there. The street gangs on the estates hate the Albanians but they have to deal with them because they control so many of the drug supply routes in and out of London and the UK."

The same detective added: "The street gangsters are constantly on alert for the Albanians coming after them. No one wants to cross them and that makes the street crews very nervy, which is when they slice people up."

UK Home Office figures state that in 2019 Eastern European gangsters committed more than one in four of all crimes in the UK. That includes nine out of ten drug offences. Balkan nationals are even the most likely of all foreigners to be prosecuted by the UK police.

This means the real top boys and their street crews on estates across London and the rest of the UK are sitting in the middle of an immigration-fuelled tinderbox. Many Eastern Europeans get into Britain using false identities, which helps to hide their criminal past.

As one London drug dealer told me recently: "We don't even know their real names. They can come in here, shoot us and then fuck off back to Albania or wherever they come from, and we don't even know how to find them again."

THE GASCOIGNE

Most Albanian drug gangsters in London keep on the move as they supply shipments of food to the street gangs. However there is one vast housing estate in east London, called the Gascoigne, which is controlled entirely by young members of the Albanian mafia, who call themselves the Hellbanianz.

The estate was built in the 1960s and occupies land which slopes south of Barking town centre down to the Thames. It's territory that today no other criminals ever dare to enter.

From the 12th floor and above of the Gascoigne Estate's high-rise blocks, there is a view of the skyline of London. On a clear day it stretches west for many miles. In the opposite easterly direction – several miles along the Thames – lie the huge container ports including Tilbury where secret shipments of cocaine are regularly offloaded through crooked customs officials.

In early 2020, I was briefly introduced to a group of Hellbanianz street gangsters by a Balkan crime vet called Darko as they stood near Crispe House, a tower block on the Gascoigne estate.

I'd known Darko for five years through another book I wrote, so he was able to vouch for me to these younger, more unpredictable Eastern Europeans. They clearly look up to Darko and insisted that he could speak to me on their behalf.

But I noticed they immediately examined me very closely as we talked on a walkway overshadowed by the enormous tower block. These young Albanians even make their own glossy drill videos with titles like "HB are ready for violence" during which they show off on social media their immense manpower and firearms posing from the multiple balconies of Crispe House.

They also post social media images of Ferraris, wads of £50 notes and gold Rolex watches to help enhance their reputations as gangsters and in order to recruit "yungers".

Not surprisingly, the Gascoigne estate has seen a steep rise in gun and knife crime in recent years. According to locals, the Hellbanianz "won" the right to sell drugs on this estate after shooting two local street gangsters dead who tried to stand up to them. As a result, this is the only London housing estate where local street gangs have stepped aside and let the Albanians take over.

Recently retired Albanian crime lord Darko told me all this as we stood with his young compatriots. Then one of them said in near perfect English: "Usually we don't work the estates. We leave it to the black kids, but this place is like a vital hub for our operation, so we got rid of them. They won't give us any trouble."

The Hellbanianz's street dealers and their enforcers mainly belong to a Mafia group called the Shqiptare, who're the dominant Albanian organised criminal syndicate. The UK's equivalent to the FBI – the National Crime Agency –

believe the Shqiptare's power and influence over London's multi-billion pound cocaine market is without precedent.

Another of the young Albanian gangsters on the estate explained through Darko: "Now we supply everything and they have to pay whatever prices we want to charge or they don't get no food."

After ten minutes, my guide Darko advised me that it was time to leave the young Albanian gangsters. He explained: "Some of them think you might be police, so it's probably best to go now."

An old British professional criminal called Den later told me: "It was all fine and dandy until the Albanians turned up a few years back. We stuck to the rules. We didn't shoot no one unless we really had to and we had a pretty decent working relationship with the street kids. But that's all turned to shit now.

Over in Albania all the signs are that this underworld invasion of London is not going to end anytime soon.

THE MOTHERLAND

In October 2019, I travelled to Tirana, the capital of Albania, to talk to crime lord Petr, whom I'd been told had recently retired after running one of the biggest drug networks in London and the south-east of England.

Petr had worked with many real-life top boys and their soldiers, so his take on the street gang-dominated housing estates of London and throughout the UK big cities was very insightful.

Petr explained: "Those kid soldiers and their top boys are not important to us. If we wanted to, we would go in and take every spot and corner from them but for the moment we're happy to let them work the streets with the drugs we've supplied.

"But that will only last for as long as they continue paying good money for our shipments. Whenever they behave badly, we make an example of one of them. They know not to fuck with us."

When I asked Petr how often he used to visit the UK before his "retirement", he admitted that he was still "active" after all: "Oh, I still live in London half the year. I use a different identity because I spent some time in prison in Albania and the British would not allow me in if I used my real name. I like life in England but I also like to be back here in Albania."

So Petr manages to control and retain his lucrative cocaine shipment business from Albania to the UK. 'It's not easy but I have many friends in high places, so I can always get my shipments through without any problems. That is the most important thing in my business."

In the Tirana bar where we met, Petr then explained in more detail about his gang and his dealings with some of London's most notorious top boys and their crews on housing estates across the capital.

"I understand these boys because they are from the slums," said Petr. "They've suffered from poverty like us Albanians. That makes them tough. I dealt direct with the street gangsters because I make more money by not using a middle man. But it is risky.

"These kids are wild and undisciplined. They often don't care if they live or die, so we always make them pay us in advance for every shipment they buy from us."

So, how does the cocaine get from Petr's homeland to London's housing estates?

Petr's eyes narrowed. He looked across at his henchman sitting nearby. Then he took a long drag of his cigarette. "I cannot tell you that, then all the scum would try to steal my drugs. Not good for business."

But Petr did admit to me during our meeting that those who transport his drugs are killed if they lose his shipments.

IN CONTROL

In London a few weeks later, one of Petr's Albanian hench-men, Carl, drove me around a notorious north London housing estate to show me how the cocaine supplied by the Albanians reaches the top boys and their crews.

We moved along a perimeter road close to a long row of dilapidated lock-up garages, mainly secured with rusting padlocks. A group of six youths outside one garage looked up as we drove past and stared hard at us.

"They're suspicious," said Carl. "Because they're on the frontline dealing with all the crap and their enemies. We don't even get our hands dirty thanks to them."

Carl revealed how a few weeks earlier he'd met with a top boy close to where we'd just driven. He explained: "He was late, which pissed me off. I got angry with him. Then he told me he'd just killed some kid who was working for one of his enemies and it had delayed him.

"He said it like it was totally normal to kill someone. Just like that. No remorse. No emotion. That's how these kids are. They have no heart and soul. That's why we have to be tough back to them."

Following the murder, the police found the body of the kid who'd been killed outside his own family's flat on the estate. It was a message from his top boy to all his soldiers. Don't rat on me or this will happen to you."

Carl shrugged his shoulders. "That's how it goes in this business."

And the Albanians are not the only gangster invaders who've created havoc in London's lethal druglands.

THE TURKS

Gangs of old-school Turkish criminals based in north London have been involved in the UK's drugs trade for the past forty years. In the 2019 third series of *Top Boy*, Turkish mafia gangsters are portrayed as still being very much part of the capital's drugs underworld as the city's predominant suppliers of brown. That's heroin to you and I.

They and the top boy gangs across north London don't like or trust each other. But following the more recent emergence of the Albanians, they've had to work together and form an uneasy truce.

One former north London street gangster told me: "The Turks think they still rule this side of London but they're growing old and starting to pull back like the old-school Brits did a few years back."

The same former gangster explained: "We took a lot of shit off the Turks for years. They looked down their noses at us and they was more racist than the British gangsters and the feds put together.

"There was this one fat boss guy with one leg. He ran the main Turkish crew, who brought in more brown than we knew what to do with.

"You see, Brown goes in and out of fashion all the time. At one stage it got popular again when the Turks stopped cutting it with so much shit. The key to selling any food to regular punters is to make sure it's strong enough to hook all the junkies in, so they'll come back for more."

UNEASY PEACE

In 2018, street gangsters on one notorious London estate held a sit-down meeting with the Turks and "words were exchanged" about their "over-cut" shipments.

"That fat guy with one leg was some evil motherfucker," explained the same former street crew gangster. "He just wouldn't take on board what we was saying. All he cared about was cutting his brown and making three or four times more in profit.

"When we explained to him how bad that was for business, he went crazy and told us to fuck off. Weapons were drawn. But we knew he couldn't cut us out completely because he needed our p's, as much as we needed his brown."

The street gangsters eventually managed to persuade the Turkish crew led by the drug baron with one leg to relent.

"But I could see from the look in his eyes he thought we was stupid," explained the same street gangster. "He wasn't happy. He didn't like being told what to do by a black man, either. But he had to swallow it."

However that peace treaty didn't last long. Within months – in the middle of 2019 – a vicious war broke out between the top boys and the Turks led by that same "bossman" with one leg.

One former street gangster explained: "It was heavy stuff. They came onto our estate with guns and blades and stuff and tried to ambush us. They was slashing at us with Samurai swords and shooting a lot of bullets in our direction."

The Turkish gang boss with one leg stayed in a van nearby watching it all. The street gang eventually forced the Turks off their territory by bringing in extra soldiers from surrounding territories in a massive show of force.

That battle helped cement the reputation of the street gangs across some of London's biggest housing estates.

A LAW UNTO ITSELF

There is one lucrative underworld territory outside London dominated by a legendary top boy that is greatly envied by many street gangsters.

Liverpool – more than two hundred miles north of the UK capital – has been dubbed by many of the criminals I've met over the past thirty years as "Britain's only independent criminal 'state'".

It's an entirely self-sufficient underworld that provides a template for the future of crime in London and all the UK's big cities. As one Merseyside professional criminal told me recently: "We run everything from the drugs to the crooked feds here and no one gets in our way."

Not even the most notorious UK-based Albanian drug gangs – who now run most food shipments to street gangs in London – dare set foot in Liverpool. And a lot of this is down to one legendary local top boy whom everyone – including some of London's most powerful street gangsters – look up to.

I first encountered Curtis Warren – street name Cocky – back in the 1980s. He is credited with single-handedly changing the face of the UK's drugs underworld. Cocky's operations were without doubt ahead of their time and the impact of his criminal activities is still felt to this day.

For the past thirty-five years, this so-called master criminal has smuggled tens of millions of pounds' worth of drugs each month into the UK.

One current day Liverpool top boy summed Cocky up when he told me recently: "This city is like one big housing estate and Cocky has been at the centre of it for many years. He ran everything that came in and went out of here when it came to drugs and other crime. And he and his posse still know every street and every alleyway."

The key to Cocky's street gang domination was (and still is) Liverpool's port facilities, which enabled drugs to arrive in the city direct from the source countries where they'd been cultivated. This cut out the many handlers, who're usually part of the drug supply chain process.

As a result, top boy crews across Liverpool today work more closely together than down in London because the entire city operates most of the time as one sole territory. That means a much wider circle of criminals with a central control hub for the city's street gangs.

Another key ingredient behind Liverpool's "crime success story" is the population. One former Liverpool detective explained: "Black, white, yellow, brown. The colour of your skin means fuck all in Liverpool. If you're a local criminal and you know how to make money, then you'll do well here."

But then this city reeks of crime. Everywhere you look, people are up to no good. It's in their blood and neither the feds or any outside gangsters have ever managed to put a lid on it.

And there is no doubt that much of this is down to Curtis "Cocky" Warren.

One former west London street gangster explained: "Cocky is the one we've all heard of, even though he comes from my dad's generation and was based in Liverpool. Cocky was black and proud of it and ruthless to the core.

"He was also the first blud to show the rest of us that we didn't need some old white stick-up merchant to supply rip-off food to us."

Control has always been the key to Cocky's operations. He was one of the UK's first street crime bosses to have crooked police officers on his payroll. Those bent cops became a crucial part of the success of his criminal empire.

EXPANDING

Cocky has never been afraid to branch out to new territories, either. The entire city of Liverpool might have been like the equivalent of the Summerhouse Estate, but he was always prepared to do business much further afield.

"That's why his story is so different from one of today's top boys," explained one former Liverpool street gangster.

At one stage, Cocky even teamed up with another big-time drug baron based in the north-east of England to give them complete dominance of the English drug market north of Birmingham, during the 1990s. This sort of amalgamation would be unheard of in today's classic top boy gangs in London and the UK's other big cities.

When Cocky's jealous criminal rivals in Liverpool informed on his activities to the feds, his reaction was simple and ruthless. A number of his rivals disappeared and it was alleged that Cocky had helped them on their way.

In the 1990s, Cocky made a move to try and dominate the entire UK drugs underworld when he travelled from Dover to Calais by ferry on a fake British visitor passport. Accompanying him was a "marketing representative" for the Cali cartel in Colombia. Cocky also had a former Liverpool fed accompanying him as his personal bodyguard.

Cocky and his associates assured immigration officers they'd only be travelling inside Europe. Then they drove to Brussels airport, where they parked their car and caught a plane to Malaga, Spain. From Malaga they went up to Madrid. Then Cocky and his accomplice took out their own genuine ten-year regular passports and flew across to Caracas, Venezuela, which just happens to share its border with Colombia.

In South America, Cocky was introduced to a man who headed up a legitimate corporation with links to the Colombian Cali cartel. Cocky then put down a £20 million deposit for two giant shipments of cocaine.

The first – of 1.5 tonnes – would arrive in Liverpool's docks the following month. The coke was to be hidden in steel boxes sealed inside lead ingots, which were not easy to slice open and impossible to X-ray. Cocky even had two more corrupt feds on hand to ensure the shipment got through.

Just before it was due to arrive, Cocky flew to Amsterdam with his ex-fed bodyguard and two associates to confirm the final details of the deal with the Colombians. Days later, another Cali cartel member flew back to Liverpool and linked up with Cocky, and the two men headed west to the docks to await the arrival of the shipment of drugs.

They used special tools to remove 500kg of cocaine, which Cocky then distributed through street gangs in Liverpool. Cocky's distribution deal guaranteed he was already in profit before he'd even flogged a gram of his coke on the streets.

A second shipment containing 900kg of cocaine left Venezuela a couple of months later. As it came into Liverpool's docklands, Cocky and his henchmen were arrested by the feds. It looked as if the law had them bang to rights this time.

But then certain serving feds – whose real identities have never been known – came forward and claimed Cocky and his henchmen were valuable informants and should be allowed to walk free, so they could put the finger on some even bigger fish.

The case against Cocky was thrown out and he was released.

Cocky went on to rule the UK's drugs underworld on and off for years despite later being sent to prison for a long stretch. His power and domination continue to be admired by many London top boys and their crews.

Cocky was recently released from prison and many believe he may well now be on the lookout for some new opportunities.

SECRET ADVISOR

While many criminals undoubtedly like to keep a low profile, the same could not be said of one of the London street gangs' most unlikely associates.

Drug baron Howard Marks worked with numerous London criminal gangs from the late 1960s onwards and never fell out with any of them. He even wrote some best-selling memoirs about his adventures in the underworld, as well as claiming to have worked undercover for UK security services.

I knew from my first meeting with Howard thirty years ago that he'd always remained active in the underworld, despite his media connections. As he told me at the time: "It's in my blood. I can't walk away from it completely."

But then Howard had singlehandedly smuggled tens of millions of pounds' worth of hash and cocaine into the UK over the previous forty years.

We last met in 2014 – just two years before he died – in a trendy pub in the middle of Hackney, east London, close to where *Top Boy*'s fictional Summerland council estate is located. He'd just seen the first and second series of *Top Boy* and said he was "blown away" by the show.

Howard explained: "I've been waiting a long time for a British TV series that actually gets it right and *Top Boy* does exactly what it says on the tin. The creator and producers deserve my utmost respect.

"It's as real as you can get," said Howard, supping on a pint and about to make himself a rollie.

"The street gangsters have been getting younger for decades. Black men in this country had been stamped on by the white professional criminals and the police for far too long.

"But it took the younger generation to say, 'We've had enough. We're taking over now', and now look at them!"

Howard dealt with the Yardies many times between the 1970s and 1990s. He recalled: "They were a ruthless organised international mafia while these kids today usually stick to their own housing estate gangs. But they learned about violence from the Yardies over the years and we're seeing the chilling result these days.

"I'm not shocked by the level of violence. These street gangs are constantly trying to send out messages to their enemies: 'cross me at your peril.' They're also under a lot of pressure from the Albanians who provide most of the shipments these days."

In 2012, Howard Marks worked as an "advisor" to one east London street gang, who'd decided to expand the hash side of their business on their housing estate.

"Hash was my main expertise by then," said Howard. "The young gangsters I met were extremely respectful towards me. They paid on time and we never had a cross word between us.

But I avoided cocaine by then, so it no doubt made it easier to deal with them."

For obvious reasons, Howard Marks refused to name the street gang he was dealing hash with but he had a prophetic word of warning when it came to the future of these real-life top boys.

"They're gonna have to watch their backs more and more because the Albanians and the Colombians may soon decide to join forces and try to take over all aspects of the London drug trade, including the street dealing.

"If you think the Yardies were cold-blooded then watch out for the Albanians and Colombians combined as one force. They have the business acumen and the same cold-blooded attitude as each other."

Howard Marks predicted that London street gangs could survive but only if they never ventured beyond the boundaries of their own estates. He explained: "The Albanians have believed for a long time that they should own many of the territories outside London. It's a tricky stand-off which can only end one way."

Howard Marks revealed that one of his closest street gang contacts had been so terrified by a killing that he'd broken the golden rule and agreed to go into a witness protection programme.

The case that Howard Marks referred to was one of the most shocking killings of an innocent bystander in east London gang history. It was committed near Marks's home in Hoxton.

Two gangsters including a notorious soldier called Bacon gunned down an innocent teenage girl in a takeaway chicken restaurant back in April 2011 when they sprayed the shop front with bullets as part of an ongoing feud between their gang, London Fields, and the notorious Hoxton Boys.

Howard explained: "I told my gangster friend to go to the feds. He was going to be killed by his own crew because they suspected he might be about to rat on them. He had no choice but to go to the police."

Today that gangster has been in the witness protection programme for more than eight years. His evidence helped convict both of the killer street gangsters, including the killer known as Bacon.

"My friend helped the feds because they gave him no choice. What those two gangsters did was unforgivable. They killed an innocent schoolgirl for no reason and they didn't even seem to care," explained Howard Marks.

"I don't usually condone ratting on your mates but this poor guy had to do the right thing."

Howard Marks' same street gangster associate witnessed other shootings and may even have participated in some himself. He only agreed to rat out his fellow gangsters after his crew's top boy threatened his family.

"He knew he had to go to the feds to protect them," explained Howard. "Eventually they gave them all a new home a long way from here."

Howard Marks told me: "This guy was just a kid caught up in a vicious underworld that he thought he had no choice but to join. Imagine how many other kids are out there with exactly the same dilemma."

YUNGERS

So London's twisted drugs underworld seeks out the youngest and most vulnerable to help it thrive.

In *Top Boy*, millions of viewers have watched the way street gang leader Dushane and his crew use children to sell their drugs without stopping to consider that what they are doing is no better than slave labour.

In 2019, the National Crime Agency – the equivalent to American FBI – reckoned the use of children for narcotics activities throughout the UK generated an income of £500 million for gang leaders across the country.

And law enforcement also considers this cold-blooded exploitation of underage children as being akin to "modern slavery". It's undoubtedly helped breed a new generation of young street gangsters who're even more prepared to spray the streets of London with bullets, blood and blades.

In series three of *Top Boy*, twelve-year-old Summerhouse resident Stefan is so worried about his mum running out of money and being deported that he starts working for Dushane's corner chiefs, Jaq and Dris.

Also in series three, new top boy Jamie's soldiers carry out carefully planned acid attacks on school kids, who're pushing food for his enemies Dushane and Sully.

In today's street gangs, the "yungers" tend to be aged thirteen to fifteen while the so-called "olders" are fifteen to eighteen. But there are also the "smalls", who're eight to twelve, often pumping their BMX-style bikes around the streets and alleyways, observing everything, including the olders.

It's all part of the infrastructure of the street gangs on many London housing estates. That "system" is deliberately kept in good working order to prevent the police from threatening these twisted druglands.

EASILY MANIPULATED

Children are often used by street gangs because the police are obliged to be much more lenient with them and jail time is also considerably less if you're under eighteen years of age.

But none of this helped onetime north London resident Gulistan Subasi, aged twenty-six. She lived in Turkey but had returned to the UK to see her young son, who was living with relatives of her estranged husband.

At 8.20 p.m. on 22 March 2010, the doorbell rang on her mother's flat in Clapton, east London, where she was staying. Footage from a CCTV camera on a nearby wall showed a short, stocky hooded figure waiting calmly and patiently for an answer.

Inside, her mother Dondu said to Gulistan: "No, daughter, we don't know who's at the door, I will answer it." But Gulistan insisted on answering it because she hoped it might be her son coming to see her on the eve of his birthday. She'd even bought him a present from Turkey.

But as Gulistan opened the door, the hooded man lifted the barrel of a snub-nosed sawn-off shotgun, squeezed the trigger and blasted her from point blank range. The gunman's face was hidden from the CCTV camera. It looked like a classic execution.

Gulistan crumpled to the floor and died seconds later in the arms of her mother, Dondu.

Estranged from Serdar Ozbek – the father of her son – she'd been due to get married in Turkey that summer. She'd even talked about getting back custody of her son.

Detective Chief Inspector Jackie Sebire later told reporters: "When we saw the CCTV we all thought it was a professional hitman. There was no hesitation and he showed no nerves."

In fact, the killer was fifteen-year-old schoolboy gangster Santre Sanchez Gayle – street-name Riot. He'd been ordered by his top boy Izak "Iceman" Billy, aged twenty-one, to carry out the hit. Both men were members of the Kensal Green Boys (KGB) gang in north-west London.

The police eventually tracked down hundreds of mobile phone records and focused on a flurry of calls on Riot's phone in the days running up to the murder.

One call was actually the contract killing of Gulistan being commissioned. Top boy Iceman even sent Riot to the block of flats to scout the location but the Iceman was careful not to mention that he was receiving £2,000 for his part in the contract killing.

Moments after shooting dead that young mother on her doorstep, Riot got into a waiting minicab and headed away from the crime scene. The driver later testified that Riot had seemed calm when he got back in the taxi. Riot was paid just £200 by Iceman for the hit.

He'd thought he'd get more money. But Riot's gang associates were impressed and he believed the killing would get him a lot of credit out on the street. Riot particularly wanted to impress older members of his street gang, including Iceman, who'd hired him for the "job".

Later on the same day of the murder, Riot even bragged about how he'd killed a "Turkish woman" to friends in Willesden, north-west London. One of those teenage mates was Ryan Hatunga.

Hatunga later said Riot even mentioned a specific security grille that covered the door of his victim's flat. One detective said: "When I heard about the grille I knew only the killer could have known about that because we'd never revealed that."

Riot was jailed for life and received a minimum of twenty years. His top boy Iceman was also given life and ordered to serve twenty-two years.

One detective said of the killer: "He's not a very bright lad. He did not have good schooling or much parental control. He was easily manipulated. In many ways he himself is a victim."

Victim Gulistan's estranged husband Ozbek was cleared of murder, as were two other men allegedly involved in commissioning the hit. But afterwards, Riot's family connections were uncovered and they disturbingly implied that murder was in his genes.

Riot's half-brother Lloywen Carty had in December 2006 been given a minimum of thirty years for the murder of twenty-seven-year-old Lee Subaran at the Notting Hill Carnival.

A month earlier Carty's half-brother Donnel Carty was given a life sentence for murdering City lawyer Tom ap Rhys Pryce, during a botched mugging in Kensal Green.

GO COUNTRY

If you ask most street gangsters the best way to make the big money the quickest from the drug game, their answer is always the same: "Go country", which is street language for the County Lines phenomenon.

Today it's emerged as the most chilling side of London's street gang activities and it relies on young children to guarantee its success.

Top boys and their crews have been deliberately recruiting underage kids to move their 'produce' between the UK's biggest cities for some years now.

That means children being recruited to transport tens of millions of pounds' worth of drugs every single week. It's reckoned that at least five thousand under-sixteens are involved in these so-called County Lines drug smuggling operations at any one time.

These "yungers" are deliberately used to get around the police's stop and search rules because they cannot be as easily arrested and detained as they're underage.

One former street gangster explained: "The younger the better, because the feds can't sling 'em in jail if they're below a certain age. That's why we use them to smuggle food and hold guns and ammo.

"A lot of crews often say the kids they use have volunteered but most of them work for us cos they're shit-scared."

But some yungers do seem to actually revel in the responsibility. One thirteen-year-old from an east London estate told me: "It's a chance to earn some real p's."

Usually this involves catching a train to a town outside London. It could be anywhere.

The same younger explained: "Then you get to a house and in that house is many people, a lot of food and probably some guns and knives too. You're there to deliver and then sell the food.

"The olders have got guns in case anyone finds out ya there and tries to come and steal the food. You gotta have protection."

Going Country means leaving that crash pad house and not returning until all the drugs have been sold. Most young gangsters will already know where the best spots are to sell drugs because they've been there before.

Originally, these so-called county lines operations revolved mainly around the London suburbs, which were considered "in the country" by urban kids. Hence the name.

But soon children started being used to transport holdalls or backpacks filled with wraps of food much further afield.

Today, the police still stop anyone they suspect of breaking the law but they do tend to be much more cautious then they used to be. "The feds don't do much," explained one gangster. "They must know we're there but they steer clear. Not enough of them to cope."

WAR WITHIN A WAR

The main principle behind going country is that once an area is identified as having a big demand for drugs then it can be exploited before the police even realise they've been there or have the courage to confront any suspected participants.

Often the police are so undermanned that street gangs frequently return to old areas without worrying that the police will come hunting for them.

In fact, the biggest risks connected to these county lines operations come from rival criminals. One west London street gangster explained: "If a rival posse tries to take over a territory then that's when there's trouble. Couple of weeks back I was in Slough selling food and this crew of Asian lads tried to shake us down.

"Guns were drawn and I thought it would really kick off. Then our top boy appears and does a deal with the Asian lads to let them work the area when we not there.

"I was surprised because it's usually not good to give up territory but this was out of our safety zone, so I guess it made sense."

But invading new territories can also mean hard graft. Another county lines gangster told me: "When you're in an area away from your home like that there is nothing else to do but sell food night and day. All the time I'm thinking of the money I'm makin' and that makes it worth it."

"It's knackering, man, you gotta be on high alert all the time. You don't know the streets like you know home.

"Then you get a few hours' sleep in dis shit house that ain't your home and then you're back out on the streets. You basically selling food around the clock."

A county lines "house" is usually akin to rundown student accommodation in a cheap rented property away from prying eyes.

One soldier explained: "Some of us are going to college in the day so we don't stay. We travel to college, do our lessons and then come back in the evening to work the streets."

The use of street names also adds to the kudos, which appeals to these young wannabes. As one former gang member explained: "You get given a name few know about, except other gang members. That bonds you even closer together."

CHILD SLAVERY CONTINUES

There is no getting away from the fact that this is child slavery. Across the globe, when kids are used like this, we're told to boycott clothes and other goods that come from factories using children.

In *Top Boy* series three, Sully quits the Summerland housing estate and heads for the coast of south-east England and sets up a County Lines-style operation from a rundown house in the centre of the seaside resort of Ramsgate.

Sully is soon running gangs of young kids as street dealers. Like so many real County Lines operations, Sully discovers he can earn big p's away from Summerland.

Back on the doorsteps of London, children as young as ten continue to be coerced into taking deadly risks selling drugs on the streets and housing estates.

Yet there's also a sense of acceptance within many of London's housing estates when it comes to the way children are being used.

Child protection agencies often can't intervene because of violent threats from the gangs that dominate such housing estates. The children themselves live in fear their families will be punished if they don't "work" for the top boys.

As one recently retired south London drug squad detective explained: "We have to address this problem one day. It's not just about drugs. This is about our standing as a so-called civilised nation. Slavery was supposed to have ended centuries ago, surely?

"We have to cut off the supply route of cheap labour to the street gangs and then gradually we might start to be able to dismantle them."

Onetime street soldier Ratboy's story sums all this up. He explained: "I started working for a gang on my estate when I was nine years old. My mum was a junkie. My dad had long gone.

"We didn't have enough p's to buy food for me and my sister. I had to go out to work and the gangsters on the estate offered me security and a family. Sure, I was scared of them but how else was my family gonna survive?"

Yet few of these so-called slave children come to the attention of the authorities. Recent statistics show that 52-55,000 children are referred to live in care in London each year but only 30,000 are put on the child protection register. "That 20,000-plus gap is the kids out committing street crimes," said one expert.

Put simply: street gangs have fuelled an 807 per cent increase in the number of child victims of modern slavery since 2014 in London.

GROOMED AND TORTURED

Increasingly violent gang initiations are also often carried out to intimidate kids into working for street drug gangs. It's nothing short of grooming and it begins from a very young age with offers of gifts, money and friendship.

In series two of *Top Boy*, Dushane mentions to his partner Sully casually that a rival gang in Finsbury Park, north London had tortured a child by taking his eyes out.

And in the real *Top Boy* world, street gangsters often use brutal tactics – including torture, stabbings and even rape – to initiate children into gangs and deal with their enemies.

In series three of *Top Boy*, Jamie is encouraged by Irish food supplier Lizzie to kneecap a crew member Jamie suspects of ratting on him. She even tells him with great relish how successful this method of punishment was when she was a child on the mean streets of Belfast during The Troubles.

Back in the real London underworld, new young recruits to street gangs are often forced to perform highly risky tasks as part of their initiation into a crew.

Just a short distance from where the fictional Summerland Estate is located in Hackney, east London, a real-life initiation attack stunned a neighbourhood back in June 2019.

Nursery teacher Christel Stainfield-Bruce was pushing her three-year-old son in a buggy along Caedmon Road, Holloway, when she was approached by a teenager.

The boy – believed to be between fourteen and sixteen – asked for directions to the nearby Emirates football stadium. But when she pointed in the right direction with a phone in her hand, he ordered her to give it to him. She refused and then the boy leaned forward and knifed her in the back of the leg before running off.

After being stabbed Christel – who is trained in first aid – wrapped her jumper around the wound and sat down on the curb and calmly called the emergency services for an ambulance.

Christel later concluded that the incident had been an initiation attack because the teen didn't hesitate before stabbing her. He also didn't try to take her phone or purse after the attack.

She said: "I had no history with this person. I was just a random target. It almost felt like target practice."

But like so many aspects of the real top boy world, it's inevitable that "family-type" relationships between yungers and street gangster bosses will eventually turn to violence. And that constant threat helps the gangsters to continue to force these children to work for them.

EXPLOITED

One mother whose son was lured into a gang this way, talked to London's LBC radio in January 2020. She said that her son was stabbed "more than twice" as part of a twisted initiation ceremony held by older gang soldiers under the control of one top boy leader.

One stabbing was in the boy's private parts and the other nearly cut a main artery in his arm. The mother of this child later recalled: "They talked about what they'd done to my son to my face when I confronted them on the estate. They made it sound like it was nothing special.

"But my son was never the same after those stabbings. He tried to leave the gang and they hunted him down and forced him to transport drugs across county lines.

"And it's not just my kid, either. I know the mothers of six other children on this estate whose children have been treated this way by the drug gangs who operate from here."

One child was attacked and was so scared of going to hospital to have his wounds treated that he almost bled to death. Another victim ended up with a blood infection that nearly led to him having his leg amputated.

The police admit they're well aware of the disturbing levels of child exploitation, but it's virtually impossible to get anyone to come forward and give evidence against the street gangsters.

Meanwhile, Albanian drug bosses continue to put enormous pressure on real top boy crews and the vulnerable kids to sell their food – or face dire consequences.

OWING BIG-TIME

In the London street gang underworld, once you owe someone a favour you *have* to repay it, and this has greatly influenced the enslavement of children to this day.

In *Top Boy*, both Sully and Dushane are regularly heard saying to younger gangsters: "You owe me big-time."

As one real-life street crew member told me recently: "Life on the street is all about pay-back. This can be emotional as well as financial.

"Crews like to say you owe them all the time, so that you can't walk away from them. It keeps you down and scared, so that you also never tell the feds anything."

But exerting this type of pressure on children can have fatal consequences. The same street gangster continued: "The kids are pushed into a corner. They fear they could be in trouble if they put a foot wrong and this makes them even more likely to use a knife or a gun when it comes to dealing with other gangsters."

And this vicious cycle of death and destruction is fuelling a disturbing new development in the netherworld inhabited by the street gangs and their Albanian food suppliers.

TAKEOVER

There is no doubt the Albanians have encouraged London's street gangs to recruit underage kids to work in county lines operations.

But at the same time the Albanians have also been secretly "conquering" entire towns and villages on the outskirts of London in order to further consolidate their own powerbase in the UK.

The Albanians have "branched out" to install their own dealers on the streets and in the parks of many provincial towns to challenge the London street gangs' County Lines operations.

These new Albanian-manned county lines-style operations include many of the old British underworld's "hunting grounds" in south-east England, especially in the traditional badlands of Kent and Essex where shotgun-toting British villains had ruled for more than fifty years.

Those same professional criminals stepped back to make way for the foreign gangs in London long ago. But many are now spitting blood about how the Albanian are trying to take over their middle England cities and towns.

One Kent criminal explained: "A lot of kids have been going across county lines with food in recent years. But now the Albanians who supplied the food have decided they want a piece of that action for themselves.

"Some of us think this is a step too far. We just about tolerated them operating in London but we don't want them on our doorstep. No fuckin' way."

There are genuine fears among many Home Counties old-school villains that a full-scale war could kick off and there would undoubtedly be casualties on both sides.

As of the spring of 2020, there remained a stand-off between these three warring factors – the real top boy street crews, the Eastern Europeans and the old-school Brits. But how long will this tentative peace last?

One former soldier explained: "It's gonna kick off one day for sure. But for the moment we all have to live with each other."

No wonder this constant round-the-clock tension has fuelled the use of lethal weapons by gangsters on both sides.

THE KNIFE EPIDEMIC

The vast sums of money that can be earned through the drug trade have resulted in many London street gangsters being obsessed with their own protection.

London's ongoing knife epidemic has been dealt with sensitively on *Top Boy* because the programme's makers needed to find a balance between sweeping it under the carpet and not glamorising it, either.

But knife crime offences recorded by police in England and Wales in 2019 were the highest on record, according to the Office for National Statistics. Police recorded 45,627 offences that year – a jump of 7 per cent on the previous year. However, the true total is likely to be significantly higher because the figures do not include all the UK's major cities

So London *is* the capital of knife crime. Offences included in the figures were homicide, attempted murder, threats to kill, assault with injury, assault with intent to cause serious harm, robbery, rape and sexual assault.

Street gangster Dayglo agreed to meet me because he is scared, even though he tries to brush it all off. He told me: "Knife crime ain't goin' away. Blades much easier to get than guns so they do the job perfectly for us."

Dayglo is nineteen now but he's been using a knife since the age of fourteen when he first started running with a street gang on the south London housing estate where he grew up.

Dayglo explained: "You gotta be armed with somethin'. There ain't no choice in the matter. If others think you're not carrying [a knife] they'll come after you."

He went on: "When I first started runnin' with a crew from my estate, they told me, 'You gotta get a blade cos then no one will mess with you.' That's what it's all about. I don't like using it but if I have to, I do."

Dayglo claims to have used his knife on at least three occasions. But he insisted he's never actually killed someone. "Usually, if ya prod it into someone's arm, they'll pull back. No real harm done and then a messy situation is cooled.

"But some kids just don't get the message, so you have to hit them harder. Ya dig? We don't wanna hurt no one. We just wanna get on with our business and then get home to our families. It's as simple as that."

Dayglo says the police never enter the estate where he lives and works. "The feds keep well clear cos we take care of our own problems in here. We don't need dem."

Dayglo went on: "This is business for me. I gotta pay for my grandma, my mum and my baby brother, so I got no choice. My dad went back to Jamaica when I was a couple of months old.

"He was into crack and that's when yer world comes tumbling down. I'm not gonna make that same mistake. I got plans."

Dayglo's "plans" involve saving enough money to quit the drug business by the time he's twenty.

"I promised my fam, I'd get out before anything happened to me. Then I'm gonna get them a nice house a long way from here where we can start our lives all over again.

"Then I'll go to college and get myself properly trained in something. I wanna real job and to start a real family one day. I've seen all the shit happenin' on this estate all me life and I don't wanna make the same mistake as many of my bluds."

Dayglo claimed he turned down a recent "promotion" inside the gang he works for, which would have helped fast track him to becoming a top boy.

"I want to be able to walk away one day," he explained. "My mates think I'm crazy but they respect me. I was surprised. I thought they'd tell me I couldn't get out, even if I wanted to."

Others I spoke to on the same estate said that Dayglo was being naïve because no one is ever allowed to just walk away from the street drug gangs.

Another teenager from the estate told me: "He knows too much about how the food works. They don't let you just walk away, in case you go tell the feds everything."

But Dayglo still insisted he'd agreed an exit strategy with his top boy by promising to live in another part of the UK as soon as he quit.

Dayglo explained: "I know it doesn't usually happen but I been a good soldier for them. I never caused them no trouble. I never lost no food either."

But others on the estate said Dayglo was being allowed to think he could leave the gang because his top boy had his eye on one of Dayglo's girl cousins. He refused to discuss that aspect of his decision.

When I tried to call Dayglo a few weeks later, his mobile had been disconnected. Then I heard that Dayglo had disappeared, just after we last spoke.

His mother and sisters still lived on the estate but Dayglo was nowhere to be found.

"He's either on his toes or they got to him," one former street gangster told me.

ULTIMATE KNIFE VICTIM

It's impossible to mention in detail all the victims of knife crime on London's gritty inner-city streets and housing estates in recent years because there have been so many.

But one chilling murder of a young would-be top boy in Leyton, east London in January 2019 typifies the cold-blooded nature of these attacks and how the backgrounds of those involved plays such a big part in this and so many other similar tragedies.

It took just fourteen seconds for a gang of street drug dealers led by an east London youth known as Maj to drive their stolen Mercedes at fourteen-year-old Beaumont Crew member Jaden Moodie; knock him off his moped; jump out of the car; stab him nine times in a frenzy; jump back in the car; and then speed off.

Maj – real name Ayoub Majdouline – was an eighteen-year-old member of the Beaumont Crew's big rivals the Mali Boys gang.

The entire attack was captured on a CCTV camera in a quiet residential street in Leyton, east London. The fictional Summerhouse Estate on *Top Boy* is located close by in Hackney.

Murder victim Jaden was one of the youngest victims of London's vicious drug gang wars. While paramedics battled to save his life, Jaden had asked for his mother and told medics he was going to take her out the following night.

Tragically, victim Jaden's gang connections had sparked a never ending cycle of violence and retribution.

When Jaden was aged just thirteen, he was handed a youth conditional caution after police seized an air-powered pistol, Rambo knife and cannabis during an altercation in Nottingham – in the UK Midlands – where he'd been living at the time.

Only a few weeks earlier, Jaden had been photographed at Nottingham School of Boxing with a smile across his face, dressed in a T-shirt and sat next to his great idol, the heavy-weight boxing champion Anthony Joshua. Once Jaden had dreamt of being a champion boxer or a fashion designer.

But Nottingham had many problems so common across the UK's big cities. There had been a series of incidents – including one in January 2018 – when Jaden's mother was threatened and forced to hand over cash on the doorstep of her Nottingham home by a sixteen-year-old street gangster.

Jaden's mother was told something would happen to her or her son if they did not pay.

She'd even painstakingly home-schooled Jaden after he was first excluded from school in Nottingham.

A few months later, the family fled to east London to escape Nottingham's gangs. Jaden – already excluded from school in the city – then enrolled down south at a school in Chingford, Essex.

His aunt Tesfa Green insisted the family had battled to keep Jaden safe. She said: "My family radiate love. We adored Jaden. I could give you a list longer than my arm of our attempts to safeguard Jaden."

Jaden was even packed off to Jamaica to spend the summer with his dad, so he could be a safe distance away from exploitative gangsters. At the same time his mother was pleading for support from children's services.

But a few months after arriving in east London, Jaden was found in possession of crack cocaine at an address in Bournemouth, on England's south coast. He'd already joined the Beaumont Crew gang who operated near his new home in Leyton and was allegedly involved in transporting drugs across the nation on behalf of older street gangsters.

In the weeks leading up to his brutal slaying, Jaden was excluded from school for once again posting gangland poses of himself on social media. Jaden was by this time at the centre of the vicious turf war between the Beaumont Crew and their big rivals the Mali Boys.

The Mali Boys from Walthamstow, in east London, had at least fifty members aged between fourteen and twenty-four, and controlled the lucrative drug trade in their territory. They were said to be raking in at least £50,000 a week selling crack cocaine, heroin and cannabis.

The gang earned its name because many founding members came to Britain as children from war-torn Somalia. Even by the violent standards of London's fearsome gangland landscape, the Mali Boys are renowned for uncompromising brutality.

A month after that, the schoolboy pleaded guilty to possession of an imitation firearm after appearing in a Snapchat video holding the weapon. The caption read: "looool don't f--- wid us please were here again."

And that's how Jaden came to be driving around east London on a moped selling drugs.

At his trial, gang member Maj Majdouline initially denied being present at the murderous attack on Jaden. But he admitted being a drug dealer. The jury did not believe him and he was sentenced to life in prison. He was the only person ever prosecuted for murdering Jaden.

But Maj and Jaden's backgrounds both provided a disturbing insight into why this cycle of crime ended in murder. In 2015, Maj's father was murdered when he was beaten with a hammer and stabbed at his flat in King's Cross, along with another man. Their killer had been at the flat buying Class A drugs. After the attack, the killer had even set fire to the flat to destroy evidence.

Maj himself was originally recruited to his gang after working as an underage drug dealer in a county lines gang transporting drugs between London and many UK provincial cities. Maj had been caught by police in possession of drugs and carrying knives. He'd even served time in jail, but had always gone straight back to dealing.

Jaden's father Julian, fifty-one, was a convicted crack cocaine and heroin dealer, jailed in 2009 after being caught in an undercover police sting.

Julian insisted he only began dealing drugs to feed his six children. But the judge who sentenced him to three and a half years in prison told him: "You were not dealing to fund your habit, you were dealing to earn a living. Dealing in drugs is a totally unacceptable way to do so. Other families manage to live on benefits."

So Jaden ended up paying the ultimate price for the sins of his father. As one of Jaden's oldest friends later said: "He was at heart still a very little boy who'd pretended to be a gangster."

Other street gangsters get wrapped up in every aspect of the "game", including the ultimate tragic ego trip of trying to become rap stars.

BLADE CULTURE

In the 2004 movie *Bullet Boy*, the entire plot revolves around one gun and the street gang tragedies connected to it. But by the time the first series of *Top Boy* came along in 2011, stabbings had taken over from shootings when it came to the majority of street gang attacks.

"Guns are obviously harder to come by than knives," explained one former south London detective. "And the way that knives now dominate the inter-gang wars on the streets of London and so many UK cities has also been influenced by how much younger the gangsters have become."

Stabbings involving young criminals have now become so commonplace on the streets of London that these attacks rarely get more than a few lines of media coverage and often don't even make it on to the main TV news bulletins.

The huge increase in knife attacks in UK cities in recent years has been sparked in part by crime bosses who're more ruthless than anything ever seen before in this country.

Drug shipment suppliers – especially the Albanians – kill with impunity if a debt isn't paid or their drugs get stolen. Today's young street gangsters know these rules only too well.

One former Scotland Yard drug squad detective explained: "All this means that there are a lot of youths out there on the streets of London and other big cities bricking it, literally. They know that at any moment, the Albanians might try and make an example of them or that a rival gang have been ordered by their Balkan drug suppliers that they must exterminate their opposition."

So knife-carrying young gangsters will use their blades without hesitation against anyone who opposes them. Peer pressure also means that street gangsters have to prove they're a match for the Albanians by wounding and sometimes killing their enemies.

The majority of knife attacks in London and the UK's major cities continue to be down to turf disputes, though. This is when gangsters encroach on territory controlled by a rival gang. As previously mentioned, in the real world of street drugs, territory is king.

One former London street gang member explained: "If you lose territory to another gang that means you lose customers. And if you lose customers then your bosses come after you.

"It's a vicious circle and many kids use knives and guns to enforce these territories because they're so shit-scared of what their bosses – mainly Albanians – will do to them if they lose any business."

THE STASHER

One-time street gangster Oddjob started carrying a blade when he was paid by a gang to stash all their weapons in a secret compartment in his mother's flat on a high-rise estate.

He explained: "Those weapons included guns, grenades and knives. I had my own knife for self-protection. It was vital. Then one day I took a grenade and decided to use it to do some fishing in a nearby river.

"I chucked it in the water and it blew up causing a big splash. But then I had to run for my life when the feds got a report of an explosion. Then the top boy whose weapons I was hiding gave me a beating for wasting the grenade."

The gang cleared all the rest of their weapons out of Oddjob's flat and when his mother found out what had happened, she sent him away to stay with a relative in another part of the UK.

"She thought the crew would kill me," explained Oddjob. "I'm glad she sent me away because it meant I never ended up joining that gang. Now I've turned my life around."

But many of the kids living on those very same housing estates continue to feel compelled to buy their own blades, usually for no more than a few pounds. It's often as easy as buying a pint of milk.

DEATH OUTLETS

Today's blade epidemic is dominated by weapons such as zombie knives, hunting blades and machetes. They can all be bought with ease at shops across London and the rest of the UK.

No wonder knives have become the weapon of choice when it comes to the chilling attacks sweeping through London and many of the UK's inner-city areas today.

The most lethal of knives are often purchased at stores specialising in fishing and country pursuits, so those businesses have become prime hunting grounds for street gang members.

I visited a fishing equipment shop in the south-east of England in early 2020 to see for myself how easy it is to buy such lethal weapons. Inside the store and on display in the front window were numerous long and serrated blades that could easily kill someone with one stabbing motion.

As one former north London street gangster explained: "Those shops are like places of beauty to some crew members. They don't have to borrow or buy expensive guns because knives work just as well and they're easier to handle.

"For ten or twenty quid you can get yourself something that will do serious damage if you stick it in someone's arm or bare skin."

The same gangster claims he's visited specific specialist shops on the outskirts of London that unofficially encourage gangsters to purchase their most lethal products.

This gangster explained: "I been in back rooms of these shops where they keep samurai swords you can buy for fifty or sixty quid."

KNIFE SURVIVOR

Some of the former street gangsters I've talked to believe that many crews would feel differently about carrying knives if they knew what it was actually like to be stabbed.

It's clear from my research inside London's modern ganglands that soldiers are expected to carry a blade for protection at all times.

Street gangster Fraz is tragically well qualified to graphically explain the role of knives inside this drugs underworld and why they have cost so many young people their lives.

I first heard about Fraz when I was visiting residents on one of east London's most notorious housing estates. Some even thought he might be dead but I eventually tracked him down with remarkable ease considering what had happened to him.

Fraz had been stabbed four times on this same estate when he lost a bag of drugs he was holding for a gang. "I was a younger for the estate crew and carried drugs from one flat to another on the estate."

Then one day, Fraz was mugged by a rival gang. They snatched the drugs and he was left empty-handed. He knew his top boy would punish him but he never expected it to be so brutal.

Fraz explained: "They jumped me outside my mum's flat on the tenth floor, hung me over the edge of the balcony and tried to make me admit I'd taken the food myself, which I hadn't."

Fraz was hung over the side of that balcony a hundred foot above the ground for almost half an hour before he was pulled back onto the walkway outside his home.

He explained: "I was lucky because in the end they seemed to believe me. I was dusted down and sent on my way."

But the following day the same top boy and two of his soldiers approached Fraz in a darkened alleyway on the estate.

"I could see from the way they were walking towards me that they was coming for me after all," recalled Fraz.

They grabbed Fraz, pushed him up against a wall and told him they thought he'd stolen the drugs on behalf of a rival gang. They'd decided to teach him a lesson he would never forget.

As Fraz pleaded with the top boy and his crew, the top boy plunged a knife into Fraz's side.

He later recalled: "I felt and heard that blade kinda squelch into me. It was surreal. I watched it going in but I didn't feel much until a few seconds later after he'd pulled the blade out. Then I fell on the pavement, blood gushing everywhere. Everything was in slow motion.

"He was standing there looking down at me as I grabbed my side and felt the warm blood seeping through my shirt."

Then the top boy leaned down and stabbed Fraz again. This time in his stomach and he felt it immediately.

Fraz explained: "When the knife was inside me he twisted it around. I could feel my insides being scraped. There was this weird noise like an air bubble bursting as I rolled around on the floor."

Then the top boy pulled his blade out and stood over Fraz for a few moments.

He then leaned down close to Fraz, who presumed he was about to stab him again. But instead the top boy whispered into his ear: "Sorry blud but it had to be done." Then he walked away.

Fraz explained: "Someone called an ambulance and they arrived within minutes, otherwise I'd have been dead."

Then – as Fraz lay in hospital recovering – he got a surprise visitor.

He later explained: "It was the same top boy who'd stabbed me. I was terrified. I thought he'd come to finish me off."

The top boy stood by the side of Fraz's bed and asked: "You alright blud?"

Then he placed an envelope on the table next to Fraz's bed and walked away.

Fraz later recalled: "It had a lot of cash in it, a few thousand. Maybe he was trying to say 'nothing personal' or maybe he wanted to make sure I kept my mouth shut."

Hours later, Fraz was visited in hospital by two police officers, who'd already been given the name of his attacker by an informant.

Fraz went on: "I thought long and hard about telling them it was him but then I thought, 'What's the point?' My family would then have been threatened – maybe even hurt or killed – and I couldn't change what had happened, could I?

"Of course the money he gave me helped. But you have to let stuff like that go, otherwise it does yer head in."

Some weeks later, Fraz bumped into the same top boy as he walked through the estate where they both lived. Fraz explained: "I was shit-scared. I thought he'd changed his mind and decided to do me for good.

"But instead he handed me another envelope with cash in it and said not to worry. I didn't know what to say. I thought about throwing the money away but what was the point of that?"

Then the same top boy told Fraz he'd made sure the feds were informed that he'd stabbed Fraz to deliberately test his loyalty because he knew the feds would try and get Fraz to inform on him.

However the top boy never tried to recruit Fraz for any more assignments after that. He heard on the grapevine that the top boy had stolen back the same amount of drugs that he'd lost during that earlier incident involving Fraz.

Fraz was lucky to survive. Meanwhile, the use of lethal weapons by London's street gangs continues and they're often passed around for multiple crimes.

GUN FOR HIRE

The casual use of firearms on *Top Boy* has sparked some unfair criticism from people who believe the makers of the show are glamorising guns.

But in the real world, firearms remain a brutal fact of life inside street gangs throughout London and many of the UK's inner cities. In order to authentically depict this, the show has to include scenes with guns.

In the real top boys' world, lethal weapons are frequently "leased out" by unscrupulous gangsters and illegal arms dealers.

Police officers I have spoken to say that often such guns end up being used on multiple crimes and the impact of just one weapon should never be underestimated.

LEYTON SLOTS, HOE STREET, EAST LONDON: 9 MAY 2017

A youth weaves and scrambles through the crowded pavement as he flees three rival gang members who're fast gaining ground on him. One of them is brandishing a Browning .756mm gun.

Suddenly two shots are fired by the gang at their target as he darts into the amusement arcade.

They miss the man and he runs back out onto the pavement and disappears into the crowds once again.

The suspects were eventually arrested and later convicted of violent disorder and one of possession of a firearm with intent to endanger life.

But the Browning was never recovered.

LEA BRIDGE ROAD, LEYTON, EAST LONDON: 29 SEPTEMBER 2017

One young person is pursued across a busy road by three armed men. One of them is brandishing that same Browning .756mm gun.

Shots ring out and a bullet from that weapon slices through the leg of their target but he keeps on running.

The gang in pursuit disperses when they hear the sound of police sirens in the distance.

The three suspects were eventually arrested but subsequently released with no further action because no witnesses would come forward and tell police what they saw.

Again, the gun they used was not recovered.

CLOVA ROAD, FOREST GATE, EAST LONDON: 30 DECEMBER 2017

Yet another altercation. This time a thirty-nine-year-old man is shot by a group of men after a heated argument.

Bullets are recovered from the scene of the crime but the assailants get away and the Browning gun that was used is not found.

WALTHAMSTOW, EAST LONDON: 14 MARCH 2018

Guns are fired in a busy street as part of a ten-year dispute between the WG and NPK gangs, who dominate this area of east London.

Innocent passer-by Joseph Williams-Torres, aged twenty, is hit by one of those stray bullets. He collapses on the pavement and dies shortly afterwards.

It later emerges that the murder had been a case of mistaken identity.

Following forensic examination of the bullets that killed Joseph, it is established that they came from that same Browning, which had "been in circulation" for a year and had been used in those earlier incidents.

However, the gun was not recovered and shortly after Joseph's killing, it's offloaded to another street gang.

TOTTENHAM, NORTH LONDON: 2 APRIL 2018

Seventeen-year-old Tanesha Melbourne-Blake is standing outside her boyfriend's mum's house with a group of friends when a car passes. Shots ring out from a Browning .756mm gun. She collapses to the pavement and dies a few minutes later.

It's a "mistaken identity" drive-by shooting sparked by an earlier brawl in a milkshake bar between rival street gangsters. Mobile phone footage of that original punch-up shows how it snowballed into the shooting, which ended with innocent Tanesha's death.

HIGHGATE, NORTH LONDON: 19 MAY 2018

A Browning .756mm gun is found by a pedestrian in a plastic bag, along with a knife and a towel next to a bin. The police then forensically connect that same weapon to all the earlier shootings featured here.

Two men and a sixteen-year-old boy were eventually convicted of Joseph Williams-Torres' murder.

Five people were arrested in connection with the killing of Tanesha – who had no connection whatsoever with gangs – but later released. Three of them were still pending further inquiries at the time of writing.

Tanesha's mother later told reporters: "Tanesha had lots going for her, a lot of goals and dreams. Everyone loved her and it broke a lot of the children's hearts as they can't believe what's happened."

So it's clear that many street gangsters continue to get away with murder. Only occasionally do the wheels of justice actually bring the guilty to book. However long that might take.

CIRCLE OF DEATH

Jamaican-born original top boy Dialo Hall shot a man dead with a long barrelled "Dirty Harry" Magnum gun in front of terrified shoppers in south London back in 2000. But he wasn't brought to justice until he was eventually extradited from Jamaica thirteen years later.

The thirty-three-year-old shooter had targeted Dennis Cowan outside a post office in Brixton. Mr Cowan, twenty-seven, scrambled behind a red post-box to avoid being shot but was "finished off" with two bullets to the head as he lay defenceless on the pavement.

Drug dealer Hall immediately fled to Jamaica where he was later arrested on other charges and jailed for twelve years following the shooting of a police officer in the island's capital of Kingston.

While serving that prison sentence, UK feds were alerted to Hall's role in the Brixton murder through his palm-print left on that post-box where his victim had cowered before being assassinated.

Hall insisted London police had framed him for the murder. But after his return to the UK, an Old Bailey jury heard witnesses describe an argument between the two men shortly before the shooting.

Hall was convicted of the murder and two firearm offences and sentenced to a mandatory life sentence.

ULTIMATE ARMS DEALER

On *Top Boy* all the gangs operating in the vicinity of the fictional Summerhouse Estate use one particular illegal arms dealer for all their black market weapons. This character is understandably careful and even talks to his customers through a bulletproof glass screen.

In 2019, I tracked down a real-life version of that arms dealer. He's known as "AK" because one of the many weapons he supplied was – and still is – the archetypal fast round AK-47 machine gun.

AK doesn't talk much about his background, although there are rumours on the underworld grapevine that AK is an ex-police officer. It's been alleged that AK once belonged to a renegade unit of corrupt detectives, who planted evidence and framed criminals and even some of their own police colleagues. But AK was never brought to justice, even after his activities were exposed when he was arrested in a raid on a central London brothel.

In recent years, AK has seamlessly immersed himself in the real top boy world as street gangsters have become among his biggest customers. He proudly boasts that he was one of the first illegal arms dealers in the UK to supply a wide range of high-powered machine pistols to street gangsters.

One source told me that AK first gained access to stolen arms through demobbed British soldiers who fought in Kosovo during the 1990s and other more recent conflicts. Some of these were allegedly taken by squaddies from the corpses of their enemies.

AK even often supplies old-style handguns from past conflicts as far back as the Second World War. Dealers like AK are exploiting a "grey area" which means antique or old weapons owned by legitimate firearms dealers are being passed on to street gangs.

AK runs his operation deep in the countryside of the home counties within a two-hour drive of London. Some weapons that he assembles have been made through buying gun components online from the US.

In 2019, police raided a factory run by one of AK's fiercest rivals where old guns were converted into lethal weapons. That weapons dealer was jailed for eight years as a result.

In recent years, the London feds have seized numerous guns including Smith & Wesson revolvers, Lugers and British Bulldog revolvers. Detectives say underworld armourers are even making their own ammunition for obsolete weapons, which have been reactivated.

One recently retired Kent detective went on: "A lot of coppers believe AK has been protected by corrupt senior officers because he could easily expose them." Some inside the south-east England underworld believe that AK's past could still one day catch up with him. But for the moment, he continues to thrive.

One London street gang member explained recently: "AK said his income has gone up tenfold since the Eastern Europeans turned up in the UK and the street gangs got powerful. He doesn't care who his customers are so long as they pay on time."

COLLATERAL DAMAGE

One of the most chilling habits inherited by many street gangsters in London and other UK cities from their predecessors the Yardies is the wholesale disregard for so-called "civilian casualties".

One former gang member explained: "Back in the day, the Yardies never cared who got in the way of their bullets. This helped them scare the population so badly that no one ever dared inform on them to any other crew or the feds."

Today, this cold-blooded underworld attitude is reflected with chilling accuracy by many of the young gangsters out on London's mean streets.

The same former gang member explained: "Many street gangs on estates are just plain mean and nasty. When someone crosses them they don't just go after the gangster, they often target his family and friends."

In July 2015, Turkish father-of-two Erdoğan Güzel, forty-two, and his friend Sonya Gencheva, fifty-one, were gunned down in a hail of machine gun bullets in a drive-by shooting in Wood Green, north London.

Later it emerged that these innocent bystanders were caught in the crossfire when a Hornsey street gang decided to take out rival gang members.

There are many examples of collateral damage involving street gangs. But these stand out for their sheer brutality and senselessness.

DEPTFORD, SOUTH LONDON: AUGUST 2018

The screams were blood-curdling as a seven-year-old child shouted for help while flames engulfed his home. Neighbours looked up in horror, unable to break into the blazing property.

By the time the fire brigade were able to break into Joel Urhie's bedroom he was already dead. His death was the direct result of an arson attack sparked by a gang dispute which he had nothing whatsoever to do with. Joel had dreamed of being a firefighter.

After the tragedy, police revealed that the gang responsible had been targeting Joel's older brother, twenty-one-year-old Sam. Sam had links to the 814 gang — an offshoot of Deptford's Ghetto Boys — and had spent time in jail for drugs offences.

EAST LONDON: SEPTEMBER 2019

Seventeen-year-old schoolboy Corey Junior 'CJ' Davis was sitting with friends on a bench when a man walked up behind him wielding a gun and opened fire. The shooting left CJ with incurable brain damage and eventually his life support machine had to be switched off.

It later emerged that he'd been shot in the head as part of a turf war between rival east London gangs Woodgrange E7 and The Beckton E6 crew.

CJ's distraught mum Keisha McLeod was taunted by gangs after the killing. They even bragged about her son's assassination online.

They also broadcast a home-made rap song with the words: 'I don't care your son's dead, I laughed when I saw you bury him.'

Heartbroken Keisha later explained: "These are the lyrics of the song. I've actually had to hear this. They just don't care."

Top Boy has featured a number of scenes with drive-by attacks by street hoods on rival gangs. In series three, Sully and his crew are even shot up on a petrol station forecourt after two young spotters on BMX bikes report a sighting of Sully and his crew, whom they've been shadowing on behalf of new top boy Jamie.

In today's real London underworld, drive-by shootings have also become synonymous with the city's urban gangsters. It's their most terrifying calling card.

WALTERTON ROAD, MAIDA VALE, WEST LONDON: DECEMBER 2019

Seven shots rang out as an eighteen-year-old youth was gunned down by a gunman on a moped in a gang-related attack.

As the driver opened fire, several young men ran from the scene. Images of it all were captured in graphic video footage from the dash cam of a nearby parked vehicle. Two loud bangs can also be clearly heard on the soundtrack of the footage.

After the shooting, six young men ran back in the direction of the car that contained the dash cam, unaware they were still being filmed. An off-duty army medic passing on his bicycle saw the injured youth on the floor and administered first aid, which helped save his life.

At the time of writing, police had not arrested anyone in connection with the shooting but at least the victim survived this time. And – as is so often the case – you can be sure that the weapon used in this attack will end up being used again.

One former west London detective told me: "This was a cowardly attack. Like so many, it threatened entire communities. The message from the gangs is to tell law-abiding citizens that they should never cross them. And often they end up killing completely innocent people who just happen to be in the wrong place at the wrong time."

STOP AND SEARCH LATEST

Today, the stop and search rules that sparked riots and mayhem back in the 1980s have been understandably watered down. The feds now need much more concrete proof to stop someone in the first place. Although many still see these controversial rules as an infringement of the liberty of individuals.

These days, citizens can only be stopped and searched without reasonable grounds if the feds suspect that serious violence is about to take place, or if someone is believed to be carrying a weapon or has just used one.

And some of today's street gangsters even reckon that the easing of the UK police's stop and search rules has actually helped them operate with even more impunity.

One recently retired south London police officer explained: "Being less willing to carry out stop and search operations has had a serious knock-on effect when it comes to street gangs and their associated violence, in particular the use of knives. They've been allowed to get away with stuff which has brought us to this place in terms of London's crime."

With today's knife crime epidemic playing out constantly in the foreground, some believe the feds are damned if they do and damned if they don't use the stop and search rules. But to put this all into perspective, the number of stop and searches carried out by police officers in England in the year up to October 2019 was still a very hefty 187,760.

Black citizens were stopped on 70,648 of those occasions. It continues to seem vastly out of proportion with the population demographics.

On London's estates, many citizens – including the street gangs – know their rights when it comes to stop and search. Yet at the end of the day, if a police officer claims to have grounds to carry out a search there is very little anyone can do about it.

In the 1980s and 1990s, so-called "personal factors", such as mode of dress or skin colour, were used as sufficient grounds to stop and search. At least that is now definitely no longer the case.

Meanwhile in today's street gang underworld, there remains a distinct lack of police on the ground in and around London's housing estates.

One retired officer explained: "We still don't feel safe in most council estates, so we spend as little time as possible in them. That's not something to be proud of. We should be able to go anywhere we want to protect law-abiding citizens but that is not the case."

Meanwhile the police also continue to struggle on all levels to crack down on drug networks, especially those run by London's street gangs.

But why is this?

THE FEDS

After the screening of the first two series of *Top Boy*, there was criticism that the police were portrayed – albeit briefly – as brutal and insensitive during their clashes with street gangsters and other residents on the Summerhouse Estate.

Smash 'em down raids by heavily armed police SWAT teams seemed excessive to many who watched the drama. Yet real street gangsters insist those TV scenes were a lot *less* violent than they are in reality.

One former gangster explained: "The feds always come in hard because they only get the occasional chance to nab us. But we don't care cos they can't really get near enough to us to stop us. We can take the pressure."

Most street gangsters pride themselves on never dropping their guard in front of the police. This ensures there are few leaks from gang members to the long arm of the law.

The same gangster explained: "Listen, the feds don't care if we live or die. And when you know that every fed who knocks down your door wants to shoot you dead then that makes you even more trigger-happy."

So despite the police's public pledges to the contrary, there's no sign that they've managed to stem the flow of narcotics into the UK and crack down on all the street gangsters who make vast sums of money from it.

BOTTLING IT

The police's failure to hit back at urban street gangsters may in part be down to a shortage of old-fashioned coppers on the beat and the reluctance of many officers to patrol housing estates.

One recently retired south London police officer explained: "It's a vicious circle. If there is no police presence in high crime areas on estates then how on earth can anyone expect the police to win the war against these criminals?"

Some police openly admit that many of the most notoriously violent real-life housing estates similar to *Top Boy*'s fictional Summerhouse have become places where the rule of law has completely broken down.

One officer told me: "We've 'given' the criminals back these places. They can get away with anything. How are we going to get those estates back into line? I don't think it will ever happen."

One former street gangster explained: "The feds can't cope with us. They're scared of us and the power we have on the estates. We could slice 'em up knowing that no one on the estate would ever snitch on us."

MISSION IMPOSSIBLE

With so few police officers on the ground, even the feds themselves admit they're fighting a losing battle when it comes to bringing most street gangsters to justice.

One recently retired London detective said: "Often our only chance of nicking these street gangsters is to stop them when they're out in a flash car. Only the stupid ones do that, so we end up taking a few kids off the streets but we never get anywhere near the real players.

"It feels as if the police are playing second fiddle to these psycho street gangsters. As a police officer, I find that mildly offensive. It looks as if we don't care, which in turn infers we're still racist in some way."

The London police's racist attitudes in previous decades have been well documented, and in fairness they've changed immensely in recent times.

The same detective explained: "But it's a mission impossible. We can't get inside these gangs because the knife epidemic has installed such fear in the local population that few citizens are prepared to stand up to these gangs.

"Imagine what it must be like to live on an estate that is effectively run by criminals? Every corner you turn, you bump into some of their gangsters reminding you that if you speak about them to anyone they will deal with you."

And throughout all this, the feds continue to confiscate knives off the street at unprecedented levels. One officer explained: "It feels as if all the previous knife crime clamp-downs never happened. We're at a constant crisis point because so many street gangsters carry knives."

Meanwhile officers in so-called hotspot housing estates in London now practise trauma medicine, so they can help stabbing victims, because there are so many. As one gangster explained: "Our game is all about territory. We protect ours carefully, which means no one can come in or out without our permission and that includes the feds as well."

One south London top boy I interviewed in early 2020 told me that many street gangsters like to think they're not big enough fish to warrant round-the-clock surveillance from the feds. "They don't care about us," said the top boy. "They got more important people to chase."

One of the few ways the police are able to monitor gang activity is through London's CCTV monitoring stations, which contain banks of screens linked to security cameras on housing estates and surrounding streets. Private security guards usually man these surveillance hubs but they're obliged to report any anti-social or criminal behaviour to the feds.

But most of the cameras used are not powerful enough to zoom in for close-up facial recognition of offenders or even the front doors of actual flats on an estate. However, they can be helpful at alerting the police to a situation that requires their attention on the ground.

So the feds have begun using some impressive new electronic surveillance "kit" in their war against the street gangs.

EARS ON TARGET

These days London's feds know that their most realistic chance of actually getting inside crime-riddled estates is through what they describe as using "ears on target" techniques.

Specific wire taps have proved virtually ineffective because street gangs are masters at swapping phones on virtually a daily basis and even often communicating through notes and meetings. They're also obsessed with regularly "cleaning" rooms of listening devices.

So in the street gang world, the police have begun using airborne drones to secretly monitor gang activities on some of the capital's big housing estates. These drones are crammed with state-of-the-art electronic eavesdropping and direction-finding equipment.

These small unmanned aircraft have been given the freedom to fly anywhere in UK airspace while monitoring criminals, which means they can soar high enough above their targets for them not to be easily spotted.

These drones even have extra-sensitive antennae that can be lowered from the machine once it is in flight to increase monitoring capabilities. Specially trained police operators on laptops back at their station or in nearby vans watch live streams of footage.

The technology on board these drones even enables the police to turn on a target's mobile phone remotely if and when required, without triggering the phone itself. This also enables them to get a fix on their targets at all times of the day and night. It doesn't matter how many mobile phones the gangsters throw away, as long as they use one then the spy in the sky will lock on to it eventually.

These secret drone surveillance operations were first launched in late 2018 when police and customs services took a joint decision to try and specifically target street gang activities. They even enlisted help from the UK intelligence services' own specialist technicians.

The blueprint for this type of operation came from the American Drug Enforcement Administration, who fine-tuned their operations against drug cartels in South America for some years.

Crucially, these drones can pinpoint the position of street gangsters selling drugs. The feds then send in "ground force" SWAT-style teams to make arrests.

London law enforcement also today focuses on specific top boy money transactions. In recent years, they've uncovered bank accounts linked to London street gangs everywhere from the Caribbean to the Channel Islands.

There are also some police officers determined not to give up trying to directly infiltrate the netherworlds of the lawless London housing estates and their surrounding mean streets.

THE UNDIES SQUAD

At the end of the third series of *Top Boy* it's revealed that a "junkie couple" who've been a constant presence on the Summerland Estate for all three series of the show were actually undercover police all along.

This same pair had been seen earlier in series three deliberately urging new top boy Jamie to strike first against resident top boys Dushane and Sully. Looking back on it, this clearly implies that the police were trying to provoke a bloody war between street crews.

But in London's real street crew world, undercover police are usually sussed out very quickly by gangs and local residents. As a result, they've been dismissively dubbed by many citizens in these deprived areas as "The Undies Squad".

In order to have any chance of success, these undercover officers need a genuine local background that provides an acceptable cover story for the gangs – as well as regular residents – so as not to give away who they really are.

Not surprisingly, these type of police operations are kept top secret. But one police officer from east London – who was involved in anti-gang unit operations between 2016 and 2018 – revealed what it was like after he moved into a flat in one of the area's most notorious estates.

He recalled: "It was fucking risky but we knew there were some huge drug deals being made on that specific estate and it was the only way we stood a chance of bringing the dealers to justice."

However it only took the street gang running the estate a couple of weeks to work out the likely identity of the "new tenant". The same undercover officer later explained: "As a single man, I stood out like a sore thumb because I had to live in that flat on my own after the female officer who was supposed to join me got injured on duty."

This officer's undercover operation quickly came to a head when someone put a Molotov cocktail through his letterbox. He explained: "I was lucky because I happened to be in the hallway when it happened and managed to put out the fire quickly.

"But I pulled out that night and no one has ever tried to infiltrate that estate since then. It's just too dangerous."

One recently retired London police contact told me how an undercover officer in another part of London had to be extracted from a notorious estate without being identified.

"There was a real danger that he might be targeted by a hitman if local gangsters worked out who he really was," explained the retired officer.

This particular officer was "snatched" during a "fake" SWAT raid deliberately carried out to make sure it didn't give away the fact he was a police officer.

The same officer later bravely requested to be allowed to move back on to the estate, so that the street gang running the estate did not suspect he was a fed. But in the end, the operation was abandoned after senior officers decided it was too dangerous.

One former street gangster explained: "The gangs are paranoid enough as it is but if any member or resident on an estate is suspected of working for the feds then he's dead meat."

PWITS

On the streets that surround certain London housing estates, "undies squad" officers in unmarked cars discreetly watch and photograph all known street gangsters and their friends and family coming in and out of those estates.

As one senior drugs squad investigator explained: "We have to do something to stop them. If the street gangsters know we're there it doesn't matter because at least that might force them to cut back on their activities."

These units are usually on the lookout for PWITS, which is the special police code for a suspected drug dealer with "possession with intent to supply". Once spotted, the undies unit usually calls in a uniformed squad car to carry out arrests separately from them, so that their secret identity is not exposed.

But the police remain convinced that a specific, concrete, long-term strategy will give them a chance of winning this war with the street gangs. They believe the key to cracking down on street gangs may lie in anti-gang task forces, or so they hope.

South London's Lambeth Gangs Taskforce is a typical anti-gang unit. Its office walls are covered with mugshots of "known and suspected" street gang members.

One of the biggest displays features the Angell Town GAS (Guns and Shanks) gang, which has sixty members. Then there is the Rockblock 150 gang, who've been locked in a war with the Siru from the nearby Somerleyton Estate for years inside Lambeth.

Rival gang members from ABM (All 'Bout Money) on the notorious Stockwell Park Estate, and of TN1 (Tell No One) and the 67s on the Tulse Hill estates, are also posted on other walls at this busy anti-gang command centre.

It's mandatory for Lambeth Gangs Task Force officers to wear stab-vests and they usually work three to a car when they're out hunting down gangsters on the streets and estates of their containment areas. Despite making thousands of arrests in recent years and securing numerous convictions for knife crime, this unit has only made a small dent in gang activities in these prized territories.

However, there are some occasions when these task force feds actually make their presence known on the streets of Lambeth.

ANGELL TOWN ESTATE, BRIXTON, SOUTH LONDON: OCTOBER 2015

The unmarked police Ford Focus had been seen regularly driving around the edge of this notorious housing estate many times over the previous few weeks. Locals often clocked the vehicle before saying warily, "Here come the Undies".

On this particular night, three plain-clothes feds – armed with CS spray (which temporarily incapacitates a person who poses a risk to others) and handcuffs and wearing stab vests – were in the Ford as it circled the estate. Suddenly a call came through about gang members massing in "TM1 territory". This was intelligence from CCTV cameras on the Angell Town estate.

Moments later, the vehicle slammed to a halt on a poorly lit street on the edge of the estate. Inside the car, the engine was still running as the feds readied themselves for what is known in "copspeak" as a "hard stop".

A group of teenagers appeared from a side alley. The feds immediately took off towards them before braking hard at the last moment and screeching to a halt alongside them. The three officers then leapt out of the car and shouted: "Stay there!"

Within seconds, the feds had their suspects up against the wall for a stop and search as a crowd of Angell Town residents began to gather. As usual, police action was breeding anger and resentment.

"What's your name?" the officer asked one suspect.

He was a young lad who looked no more than thirteen.

"You wanna know my name?" shouted the boy. "My name is FUCK YOU."

The police handcuffed the boy and put him in the police car while they checked his background.

Meanwhile, teenagers on bikes weaved around and showed the police "the old Angell Town A symbol". Holding down two fingers and provocatively sticking their thumb through the middle to make both an "A" and an upside-down crude "fuck you" sign.

It turned out the main police suspect's three phones did indeed belong to him and he was just fourteen years old. He was released without charge. The youngster then strutted off, swearing under his breath, looking defiant and victorious. Often the feds are deliberately "played" like this, so that other drug-related activities can continue nearby without interruption.

But it's not just young street gangsters who try to intimidate the feds' undie squads whenever they swoop in on an estate. Often indignant mothers fearlessly face up to them as well. And some of those parents even claim to be on the side of the police while actually diverting attention away from other crimes which their children are committing.

One mother on a notorious east London estate summed up the "them and us" mentality: "My boy's fourteen and he already knows who the undies are. He hates them. We all hate them because mostly they arrest the wrong people."

And when police officers try to show a human face while dealing with youngsters on the edge of this criminal netherworld, they can unintentionally put those children's lives at risk.

In late 2019, an officer befriended a needy teen on an east London estate, whose mother had just died. A few days later, the same boy was stabbed by street gangsters who thought he was working for the police because he'd been seen talking to that one officer.

No wonder police interaction with street gangsters remains virtually non-existent.

Meanwhile the most fearsome London street gangs sometimes deliberately target police officers to send out a message to their rivals that they will strike anyone who dares to take them on.

GYE HOUSE, SOLON ESTATE, SANDMERE ROAD, CLAPHAM, SOUTH LONDON: SUNDAY, 3 APRIL 2016: EARLY MORNING

The police usually avoid middle of the night visits to housing estates in case they end up sparking shootouts or causing mass riots. But on this occasion, two plain-clothes detectives were in pursuit of two suspects who were weaving through a myriad of alleys on the edge of this very gritty estate.

Suddenly, one of them turned and pointed a gun in the officers' direction. The youth then opened fire, discharging at least one shot. Neither of the officers was hurt and a twenty-four-year-old man was later arrested on suspicion of possession of a firearm with intent to endanger life.

But a lesson had been learned. One former detective later explained: "It's sad to admit but it just isn't worth taking a chance and going on an estate unless you have a lot of firepower."

However the perception of the police as always being the enemy is sometimes unfair. The writers of series three of *Top Boy* tried to address this in one scene when a Muslim woman is seen being arrested for shoplifting. Two young police officers decide to pay the £10 for the value of the nappies she stole, much to the disgust of the racist owner of the shop.

But there are other feds who give law enforcement across London a bad name.

FAT FEDS

On *Top Boy*, corrupt police officers don't get many mentions in the criminal netherworld created by the makers of the series.

In London's real underworld, street gangsters until recently usually relied on older professional criminals for inside knowledge of the police's alleged dirty habits. However today some crews on big estates have started directly paying crooked officers to help ensure their operations run more smoothly.

As one former south London drug squad detective recently explained: "Corrupt police are a fact of life. The police themselves might try to play them down and the criminals may not like having to deal with them. But they're here to stay."

Recently, I interviewed a police detective known as H, who received one of the longest ever jail sentences for corruption.

H explained: "I had my own drug habit and a family to support, so I started looking around for 'new customers'. I must have been mad but I decided that street gangs on the estates could do with my services.

"I caught a few young gangsters red-handed and once they was down the station I made it clear that unless they used my services, I'd fix it so that many of them ended up going down even for stuff they hadn't done.

"They soon spread the word to their fellow gangsters. We held meetings and one crew agreed to pay me a monthly retainer to keep them informed about all important police activities connected to their estate."

H himself was even honey-trapped by his street gang paymasters after they secretly filmed him having sex with a prostitute and taking drugs.

"I walked right into it and I guess I deserved everything I got. They squeezed me dry and I ended up being caught red-handed taking a bribe, which flagged me up to the anti-corruption boys and I was fucked."

H eventually went to jail but claims that other crooked feds soon stepped into his shoes.

"Bent cops are becoming the lifeblood of a lot street gangs these days. It's all about money. As long as criminals are prepared to pay, they will find bent coppers to give them important info."

ONLINE STARDOM

Social media's role in the ramping up of violence and retribution by gangs on London's estates and mean streets sums up the negative attitude that dominates the lives of crew members.

London's street gangs often threaten their enemies and rivals from a safe distance, thanks to online platforms. Angry personal remarks on social media are posted in the heat of the moment.

However, these broadcasts further fuel feuds out on the actual streets as many social media posts encourage violence and even murder between rival crews. As a result, social media has greatly contributed to the ever-soaring rate of violent crime in the capital. In recent years, there have been months when the UK capital topped New York for violent crime, nearly all of it related to street gangs.

A classic example came in 2017 when fifteen-year-old Jermaine Goupall was knifed to death in south London's Thornton Heath during a feud between rival gangs who'd posted mocking videos on YouTube.

As one expert on social media connections to crime recently stated: "These gangs don't seem to see any distinction between on and offline. That includes violence which used to be seen only by people in the street but is now being shared online. That's providing the impetus behind exaggerated behaviour and retaliation."

There is no doubt that shame is another key cause of the social media-inspired violence between street gangs. When footage of a gangster being beaten up in front of five people is posted and shared with thousands of others it amplifies the fury.

Often street gangsters take enormous risks posting footage of themselves showing off cash, drugs and weapons, seemingly not caring that they are broadcasting their crimes to the outside world.

In December 2019, London police launched a new unit of officers to comb social media to try and predict outbreaks of violence and gang crime. They primarily access YouTube, Snapchat, Instagram and House Party.

The unit – codenamed Project Alpha – was soon preventing "threats to life" and even helped stop a string of copycat robberies targeting JD Sports.

One former street gangster explained: "Social media is stoking all this. These kids film everything as if it's a badge of honour to show the world. That then sparks even more violence."

Some street crews even resort to using footage to blackmail their enemies. The same street gangster explained: "I know of crews who secretly film rival gangsters having sex and then threaten to post that footage on social media in order to make those enemies gangsters help them."

"That ramps up the threats even more and creates a combustible atmosphere that can only end one way – in violence."

THE CYBER TRAP

A lot of the kids who become street gangsters are poorly educated, vulnerable and bitter about how they came to have no choice but to join crews and commit crimes.

But on social media, they can lap up a constant diet of local gang rap videos aimed specifically at them. These show wannabe gangsters, some even apparently armed. This type of footage undoubtedly helps to glamorise the "gangster life" and acts as a recruitment tool for many street crews.

Some youngsters are lured into gangs with promises from top boys and their crews that they can feature on a rapper's YouTube video. These same videos are then often used to taunt other gangs, which often ends with rounds of reprisals. Moscow17 gang member and self acclaimed rapper Siddique Kamara – known as Incognito – and his drill rapping band-mate Rhyhiem Ainsworth Barton both fell into this trap and paid an awful price for membership of a street gang.

On 1 August 2018, wannabe top boy Incognito was stabbed to death just yards from the spot in Wareham Street, Camberwell, where his bandmate Barton had been shot to death in May that same year.

The Moscow17 gang had been in a longstanding feud with Zone 2 from neighbouring Peckham for months. They both operate in the heart of the borough of Southwark, which has the second highest level of knife crime in London — with almost a thousand stabbings in 2019.

SCARZ

Some young gang members think they're so talented as rappers that it makes them invincible killers. They even boast online about their crimes by creating a cyber "footprint" which could one day lead their enemies and the police to their doorstep. By building up social media followers they fall into the classic trap of believing their own publicity.

Teenager Vasilios Ofogeli called himself "Scarz" on YouTube and his onscreen drill clashes garnered a significant following on housing estates all over London and the South East. But in August 2019, Scarz – then aged just sixteen – clashed with twenty-one-year-old Andre Bent during a brawl following a grime and drill clash at the Gallery nightclub in Maidstone, Kent.

Mr Bent from Lambeth, south London, had been out celebrating a friend's birthday on the night of the attack. They'd watched rapper MoStack perform at the club. Father-to-be Mr Bent was due to start university a few weeks later to study business.

Violence broke out after MoStack's entourage left the club's VIP lounge just before 3 a.m. Shortly after this, Scarz stabbed Mr Bent, as well as Lucas Baker, Patrick Silva-Conceicao and Joshua Robinson, with a large machete-style knife. Mr Bent was so badly injured in his chest that he bled to death within forty minutes of the attack.

Police quickly traced Scarz's home address from rap videos he'd posted online. But he'd fled to Greece hours after the murder. Kent police then discovered the weapon he'd used during a search of a neighbour's garden. When Scarz returned to the UK later in 2019, he was arrested at Stansted airport.

Scarz was convicted of murder at Maidstone Crown Court in March 2020. He was also found guilty of two counts of attempted murder, and wounding with intent.

OLD SCHOOL

Many of my previous true crime books have centred around London's old-school criminals whose past is steeped in underworld history.

A very small handful of those same veteran gangsters have even formed surprisingly close bonds of friendship with the street gang crews who run London's council estates and the surrounding streets.

In series one of *Top Boy*, Dushane latches on to elderly Irish drug boss Joe, who heads up the gang that supplies the Summerhouse Estate with its food.

Back then in 2011, street gangs relied on old-school drug suppliers like Joe or else there'd be no food on the table. Full stop. Then the crews and their top boys' powerbase would collapse and London's entire supply network would start to crumble. But it was an uneasy relationship punctuated by violent flare-ups, underlying racial tensions and a general mistrust of each other.

Some of these old-school gangsters were the same characters who'd been involved in helping police crack down on the Yardies years earlier.

I was introduced to veteran gangster Baz during a tense meeting on the Costa del Sol back in 2004. He was then one of the most familiar criminal "faces" in south-east England. I was interviewing him about his rumoured role in the hitman killing of a London underworld crime boss near Marbella.

Then his name popped up during my initial enquiries into London's *Top Boy* world. I heard that he'd at one stage provided drugs to a number of street gangs, so I persuaded him to meet me once again.

"They was complete fuckin' chaos," explained Baz, smoking a king-size cigar and supping a vodka and tonic as we sat in the corner of a quiet pub in Kent. "The kids from the estates were running the street dealing by that time and they'd learned to be cold as ice from the Yardies.

"They were also arrogant, unreliable and trigger-happy. When I met the main top boy on one really big estate, I had to pull a shooter out and dent his forehead before he'd agree to my rules.

"And when I pulled that shooter on him, he didn't flinch. He just coolly answered all my questions and we got down to business."

Baz and this particular top boy worked together for almost two years without any comebacks or problems. "It was as sweet as a nut," recalled Baz. "Then this kid decided he wanted to make more money.

"But instead of thrashing out a new deal with me, he went straight to some other slags and got his food for half what I was charging him. I got mightily pissed off.

"The rule of this game is you don't drop your supplier without a very good reason and you always give him or her a chance to drop their prices first. He didn't do any of this."

Baz decided to make an example of his disloyal top boy, otherwise other customers might follow suit and try to pull out of their drug shipment deals with him. He explained: "I needed to do something big to tell everyone I wasn't a pussy."

So Baz and three henchmen kidnapped the top boy and one of his soldiers and held them in a lock-up just south of the Thames. "I didn't want to do it but I had no choice. I needed to get my reputation back."

Baz explained: "That top boy and his mate swore they'd kill me if they ever got out alive. I laughed cos kids are always sayin' stuff like that and I had his life in my hands at that moment."

But Baz didn't realise that this top boy's crew were already on his trail.

He explained: "He'd been smart enough to have his mates tracking his car at all times and one of their spotter kids had seen us snatching him on the streets. They even knew where we were holding them."

The top boy's crew raided the lock-up and a shoot-out ensued. The top boy and his henchmen escaped.

"I'd fucked up," recalled Baz. "Now I was in deep shit. So I made the biggest decision of my life. I contacted the top boy and said I'd give him a shipment of coke free and then I'd shut down my operation and he could take over the supply chain, which would mean he could get his coke even cheaper.

"For a couple of days this top boy went away and thought about my proposition. I was convinced he'd turn it down and then there would be a bloodbath.

"But in the end, he agreed to the deal on condition I quit the area immediately as promised and stopped running drugs for anyone. I'd had enough anyway, so the timing was perfect."

Within two weeks, Baz the British old-school villain had retired to his holiday villa in Tenerife and the top boy on that estate was on course to becoming one of the richest and most powerful street gangsters in London.

BORN SURVIVOR

I've known old-school London criminal Tone on and off for more than twenty-five years and he proudly calls himself "a born survivor". We first met when he was linked to the gang behind one of Britain's biggest ever armed robberies.

Tone is another unlikely underworld vet at the centre of the spider's web of criminality that feeds many of London's street crews. Although he likes to stay low-key, there is no getting away from the fact that Tone is one of the most successful full-time drug smugglers in south-east England.

He's supplied drugs for everyone from crooked police officers to Irish terrorists to Eastern Europeans.

Now aged sixty-nine, Tone first started running lorry-loads of hash from India and Afghanistan back in the mid-1970s. His transport company in the UK Home Counties has been running drugs ever since.

On the legitimate surface, Tone's firm handles fruit and veg imported from many countries in Europe and beyond. But hidden beneath some of those shipments are millions of pounds' worth of drugs, primarily cocaine. And Tone has somehow survived the ever-changing face of UK crime, which led to him supplying vast shipments of food required by London street gangs.

"I get on fine with all of them," explained Tone. "I'm a professional. I don't care who I deal with, as long as they pay and don't gimme any headaches."

Twenty-five years ago, Tone even worked with the much feared Yardies.

He explained: "They wanted to use my smuggling routes up from Spain, so I teamed up with a posse from Wembley.

"My old-school villain mates back in Kent and Essex were appalled that I'd work alongside the Yardies, who'd forced a lot of them out of the drug market.

"But the Yardies never once tried to double-cross me, which is more than can be said for some of the old-school villains I dealt with in the early days."

Tone's smuggling operation is greatly reduced in size from the old days in the 1980s and 1990s, and today he uses just five lorries. "That suits me fine," he explained. "I'm still making good money. It's better to stay small these days cos then you don't flag yerself up so easily to the cozzers [police] and other villains."

Tone went on: "I'm an old man now in a much younger man's profession so I'll probably just do a few more runs and then quit while I'm on top."

Tone is part of a carefully oiled "system" that continues to feed London with shipments of illicit narcotics, which keep the wheels of the UK capital's drugs market turning.

"I keep well away from gangsters when I'm off duty, for good reason," he explained. "If I bump into any of them we ignore each other."

But even tactful Tone has sometimes found himself at the centre of a tug of war over his drug smuggling services. "One notorious street gang wanted me to stop working for one of their rivals. It got pretty heavy.

"They tried to ambush one of my trucks when I was driving through Kent up from the channel ports. But I'd been tipped off about it and had three armed henchmen inside the truck so that when this street gang ripped open the back door they got one hell of a surprise and ran for their lives."

JUST BLOCK IT OUT

Sully on *Top Boy* often veers onscreen from tearful emotion to cold-blooded killer in seconds. It's probably why actor Kano has been so acclaimed for his magnetic portrayal on the TV series.

But there is one phrase Sully used after yet another killing with Dushane alongside him which resonates with many real-life street gangsters: "Just Block it Out."

For in those four words lies the key to how so many real-life street gangsters operate.

One former street crew member explained: "That phrase resonates so much with me. I remember the first time I was told by my top boy to beat a guy up because he owed us money for drugs.

"I was only sixteen and I wasn't a violent kid, so it was kinda hard for me to get up the courage to hurt someone. My top boy could see the reluctance in my face. He knew I didn't want to do it.

"Then he looked me in the eye and said: 'Don't think about this kinda stuff so much. Just do it. Nothing gonna happen to you.'

"The weird thing is I felt so reassured when he said that. He was my family and I trusted what he'd just said. So I got this kid and beat the shit out of him and I didn't feel a thing."

Real top boys pride themselves on rarely getting caught by the feds, but what happens when they and their crews end up in prison?

LOCK-UP

TV top boy Sully's ability to thrive inside prison is there for everyone to see at the start of series three of the hit drama series.

He shares this attitude with the UK's old-fashioned, post-war professional criminals, many of whom used to run London and prided themselves on how they coped with lock-up.

One of them explained: "We always accept our sentences as part of the job. That means making the best of your time inside to plan and scheme things to do once you're out again."

One former prison governor explained: "The street gangsters are similar. They stick to themselves when in prison. Other inmates cross them at their peril but they

don't cause much trouble for the staff. They're more inter-
ested in planning the crimes they intend to commit once
they're released."

Street gangsters stick to a strict code of conduct in jail.
One former gang member explained: "Gangsters inside
usually only link up other crew members in the same prison,
unless they have a specific beef with each other from something that happened on the outside. Then they form a mobile
unit that no one else would dare take on."

At west London's Wormwood Scrubs prison, street gangs
regularly fly drones packed with drugs into cells of imprisoned fellow crew members.

Those street gangsters then supply drugs to other
inmates in much the same way they do on housing estates
on the outside.

One former inmate explained: "The same rules apply.
If you cross a top boy or fail to pay a debt, he will send his
soldiers after you inside."

But more surprising is that street gangsters are sometimes being used by UK prison authorities to help solve
inmate problems inside jail.

One former officer at a UK maximum security jail recently
explained: "We had huge problems with radicalised Muslim
terror offenders in one closed prison. They'd virtually taken it
over and turned it into a no-go area for other inmates and staff.

"So we approached a street gang leader in another prison
who had connections to some of the Muslim inmates. We
knew they were very respectful of him. So we promised he'd

get his sentence reduced if he agreed to be transferred into that prison to help sort out the Muslim inmates.

"It turned out they were in awe of him because he'd worked alongside them on a number of county lines operations on the outskirts of London before they were all imprisoned."

Within a month of being transferred into the prison, the real top boy had persuaded the Muslim inmates to step back and allow staff to retain control of the prison.

The same prison officer later explained: "We took a big risk putting him in there and we could never have admitted doing it in public. But it worked and for that we should be grateful to that gang leader.

"Reducing his sentence by two years was a small price to pay for re-taking control of that prison."

But back in the outside world, those who have the courage to stand up to street gangs sometimes pay a terrible price.

THE WAR ZONE

Top Boy and its movie predecessor *Bullet Boy* try hard not to sugar-coat the street gangster life on London's housing estates. But neither drama has been able to fully reflect the impact that street gangs have on ordinary law-abiding citizens.

In 2017, I lived close to an estate in west London which had evolved into a world within a world where few people apart from residents dared to enter.

There were rumours that some who'd stood up to the street gang running the estate had disappeared. It was virtually impossible to go anywhere without being stopped and searched by those young gangsters .

Others in my neighbourhood claimed the police had completely given up patrolling the estate.

Then I heard about a brave teenager called Fido. He was about to take his A-levels and had plans to be the first member of his family to go to university. But he told family and friends he was outraged at how the gangsters had taken over and pledged that one day he would force them off the estate. No one believed he could do it but there were genuine fears about what might happen if the estate crew heard about Fido's dissent.

One day Fido was stopped by three knife-wielding gang members on a narrow estate walkway and forced to empty out his pockets. They stole all his cash and phone and beat him up. Many other residents took it as a warning to him and others on the estate to keep quiet.

Fido's brother Rani later explained: "Fido went to the feds to complain. Surprise, surprise, they did absolutely nothing. Fuck all. They didn't even come on to the estate to interview the gangsters who mugged Fido, even though he told them their names."

But Fido refused to back down. A couple of days after he'd been mugged, he confronted one of the same gang members on the estate and they had a vicious fight. Fido won and demanded a meeting with the top boy of the estate's street gang.

"We all tried to stop him," explained his brother Rani. "But Fido was on a high from beating that gangster up and wouldn't listen to a word we said."

Two days later, Fido was found dead from knife wounds in an alleyway on the edge of the estate.

His brother Rani recalled: "What a waste of a life, and it scared everyone on the estate even more. No one even dared mention Fido's name in case the gangsters came after them."

A few weeks later, the gangsters who murdered Fido hinted at what they'd done in a post on social media.

Fido's brother Rani explained: "They didn't actually admit they'd done it but they made it clear that anyone else on the estate who stood up to them would end up suffering the same fate."

THE REAL P'S

When smooth-talking young gangster boss Jamie agrees in series three of *Top Boy* to handle a vast amount of food each month from his suppliers, even his crew are worried that he's stretching himself.

But Jamie's prepared to take the big risks, despite his young age. No wonder many reckon the real top boys of this world could have been captains of industry if they'd taken a different path out of their childhoods.

It's believed that most top boys on London estates earn in excess of £20,000 a month and their soldiers are usually on between £5,000 and £10,000 a month *minimum*.

One former street gangster explained: "Selling drugs is no different from any business. That might sound pretty obvious but, believe me, there are many occasions when those simple rules are not adhered to and that's when it all turns nasty."

These golden rules include good marketing, which means making sure that both customers and enemies always know there are plentiful supplies in stock and also that if anyone steps out of line then they'll end up maimed or injured.

Then there is good word of mouth, which helps ensure that people are constantly talking about the quality of the food. This creates a buzz which many drug users cannot resist.

And lastly there is good product. Most narcotics – especially cocaine – are "stretched" in order to maximise profit, but successful drug dealers pride themselves on ensuring their product is still potent enough to hook in customers to guarantee they come back for more.

These rules usually apply to dubs – cocaine – because that is the biggest selling and most profitable drug for street gangs. But the most old-fashioned drug of all still helps street crews to tick over when the dubs supplies run short.

NO SMOKE

In series one of *Top Boy*, mum-to-be resident Heather is running an illegal marijuana grow in her flat in the hope it will make her enough money to one day leave the Summerhouse Estate.

In the real street gangs underworld, crews are getting their supplies of cannabis here in the UK. In 2019, the police uncovered at least ten thousand illegal cannabis "grows" in the UK with the largest concentrations located in West Yorkshire, Greater Manchester and the West Midlands.

In the summer of 2019, one street gang from a notorious south London estate raided a hash farm in Kent which was being run by an Albanian gang. However the Eastern Europeans had boobytrapped the area around the farm. As a result, two of the street gangsters were maimed for life by explosions as they tried to break into the farm.

The street gang fled empty handed and a few days later, a crew of Albanians ambushed the same crew on the edge of their estate and severely punished them.

One street gangster explained: "That posse was hurt very bad by the Albanians and the message got out that no one should ever try that again."

Meanwhile, the UK's home grow "business" continues to thrive. More than a million cannabis plants were recovered by police in 2019 and it's estimated that home-grown cannabis today supplies 80 per cent of the UK's total commercial demand.

British Gas – now a major supplier of electricity – has formed a special task force to tackle the hash growers after a huge upsurge in the use of power-draining hydroponic equipment to produce marijuana indoors without soil by pumping nutrients directly into the roots of the plants.

"Home grows" have become so widespread that the criminals behind these operation are believed to be stealing up to £100 million of electricity every year to fuel the sophisticated lighting systems needed to encourage the drug to grow. They do this by connecting up their power supplies to legitimate neighbouring electricity lines.

No wonder that today – with average prices of £21 per quarter ounce – the commercial and personal consumption markets for home-produced pot in the UK continue to boom.

THE BRIEF

Lawyer Rhianna – played by actress Lorraine Burroughs – appears in series two as top boy Dushane's legal rep who also becomes his lover.

In the real underworld, lawyers who represent street gangsters during police interrogations play a pivotal role in the aftermath of arrests. These briefs – as lawyers are often referred to – usually work for professional criminals from further up the food chain. They pay for lawyers to represent their street gangster associates for good reason.

The police are obliged not to draw any obvious conclusions from the background of these legal reps, thanks to strict confidentiality rules when it comes to the legal profession.

As one former detective explained: "It's very frustrating for the police when a certain lawyer is on the payroll of a criminal. Yet here he is defending the interests of a young street gangster, who claims he's innocent."

The feds also claim that such lawyers can sometimes be used to convey messages between gangsters and their criminal paymasters. One former drugs squad detective explained: "Most briefs are 100 per cent honest and law abiding but sometimes you get these slippery types who would sell their own granny, and when they're representing a criminal, you know you've got a problem."

No wonder many real-life police officers resent the way that these types of lawyers move seamlessly between the so-called normal world and the subterranean activities of their underworld clients.

One detective explained: "This is a huge problem because one of the keys to cracking any case is to cut off the line of communication between a suspect and the criminal boss who is behind him."

Some lawyers have been known to secretly threaten young gangsters on behalf of their criminal paymasters following an arrest, to ensure they're not tempted to help the police.

One of Britain's most renowned criminal lawyers explained: "It's crucial that a lawyer does not cross that thin line between a client and his "professional activities", whatever they may be. This may seem obvious but I've noticed more and more lawyers getting too close to their criminal clients.

"I even know of some lawyers who've accepted large amounts of hospitality from criminal clients. It's a dangerous game because professional criminals are often very manipulative characters.

"They want to own you in every sense, even if you're not actually corrupt. No lawyer should ever consider a client to be his friend. That's a golden rule in my profession."

But there's one more significant golden rule when street gangsters are interrogated by the feds. It's been around in the underworld since before most housing estates were even built.

NO COMMENT

A standard "no comment" response from suspects during police interrogations has been the staple diet of TV crime dramas for more than half a century and *Top Boy* is no exception to that rule.

In the real world of London's street gangs, this type of two-word response following an arrest is also commonplace.

As one former street gangster told me: "If the feds haul you in, you gotta stay quiet. Replying 'no comment' to any of their questions is drummed into us from an early age."

This staple "no comment" response is actually a relic of the London of the 1950s and 1960s when professional robbers ruled the capital's streets and the police were said to be much more corrupt than they are today.

Back then, crooked detectives were constantly being accused of making up false confessions by criminals in order to secure prosecutions. Hence a "no comment" response during a suspect's interrogation became a necessity to avoid being framed.

One recently retired street gangster insisted: "It's the same now as it was back then. The feds will pull any trick to try and nail you, so you have to be real careful after you get arrested. Saying 'no comment' is the best way to deal with that."

MULES

There are some desperate people lured into working for street gangs, who are in many ways the ultimate victims of London's drug crime epidemic.

Back in the 1990s, a large number of impoverished women were recruited by Yardie gangs to fly into the UK having swallowed vast numbers of sealed bags of cocaine. They were known as "mules" but that doesn't reflect the high-risk elements of what they did.

Many presumed this illicit practice had disappeared some years ago. However today's street gangs often top up their supplies of dubs by paying mules to bring in food independently of their main supplier, in a bid to make even more p's.

Bags of cocaine are often carried in small, concealed kilogram quantities by usually female couriers on commercial flights that arrive in the UK. The dubs is sometimes strapped to the waist or legs or hidden in bags. But most of the time it's swallowed in pellets and concealed in the body. There are immense health risks involved and, naturally, the street gangsters reap vast profits from the misery of these otherwise innocent women.

These mules are often drug addicts and poverty-stricken single mothers who've been deliberately hooked on free cocaine by gangsters. Their families back home are also threatened with harm if they lose the drugs or inform the authorities.

If a mule is arrested then the street gang bosses usually cut all links, leaving the mule to stand trial for trafficking alone without any support, too terrified to name anyone to the police in case their families suffer.

London's most successful mule posse is known as the "Bling Bling Gang" thanks to their luxurious lifestyles and obsession with designer labels. This crew of women have smuggled £50 million' worth of cocaine into London using mules for at least the past decade. That dubs is often "stepped on" and stretched into vast numbers of crack bags to boost the profits for the street dealers on the housing estates and mean streets of London.

Most mules often come from the smaller Caribbean islands and the poorest countries in West Africa. They usually fly into European cities such as Paris and Amsterdam. There the drugs are then handed over to London-based mules who've flown in on planes, ferries, buses and trains. Three mules – completely unaware of each other – are usually used on each flight and street gang bosses often deliberately "lose" one of those mules to customs or police.

"They let the feds know about one carrier in the hope it will leave the way clear for the other two," explained one former street gangster. "This is a sacrifice to divert attention away from the other mules and it usually works."

Favourite arrival points in London include the Eurostar terminal at St Pancras and Victoria Coach Station. Usually young gangsters are waiting there to meet their mules. The food they carry is then extracted from their bodies with a combination of methods including All Bran and cod liver oil. Often the same mules are then used to take suitcases brimming with cash back to the Caribbean or Africa to be filtered through offshore banks.

In 2015, a British pensioner was jailed for ten years for trying to smuggle almost £1 million' worth of cocaine into the country in her mobility vehicle.

Customs officers at the Kent Channel port of Dover found the drug in the old lady's specially adapted car after she arrived from France. This same elderly woman smuggler was found to be suffering from cancer when she was arrested.

Between 2013 and 2016, more than six thousand drug mules were arrested at Amsterdam's Schiphol International Airport or in the city itself.

One single flight to Schiphol from Ghana, via Morocco, was said to have carried thirty-two West African women, all of whom had swallowed cocaine packets or concealed them in their luggage.

Around the same time, a Nigerian mother with five children, Abosede Fehintola, fifty-seven, was jailed for eight and a half years for trying to smuggle £500,000 of cocaine through London's Stansted Airport in her suitcase.

It's reckoned that nine out of ten mules who cross into UK territory every day of the week are not apprehended. And there are believed to be dozens every day.

Today, many street gang crews often also home in on vulnerable women living on London housing estates in order to use them as mules. And there are other, even more innocent and vulnerable, people suffering on London's real frontline.

TO SIR WITH HATE

In the first series of *Top Boy*, a teacher is knocked to the ground by a street gangster when she's trying to protect one of her pupils in the school playground.

It's a startling scene because it shows how the street gang underworld has crossed over into a school that is not even part of the Summerhouse concrete ghetto.

In the real top boys' world, there have been numerous incidents in recent years inside London schools when pupils have been beaten up by gangster-linked fellow pupils. Teachers are even attacked by pupils aged as young as eleven or twelve on a regular basis. These attacks are often carried out on behalf of top boys to send a message to the family of anyone who owes the gangsters money for drugs.

Some gangsters in their early teens even carry large amounts of cash around with them at school for top boys, who use them as "mobile banks" if and when they require cash. These same teens sometimes even upload footage of themselves from social media showing them punishing those who cross them as a warning to anyone not to challenge them.

There have even been media reports in recent years of children as young as eleven coming into schools with knives.

One supply teacher recently explained: "These gangster kids come in here as if they own the place. They strike terror into many of the other pupils and then they disrupt class."

Some London schools have installed panic buttons following incidents where members of staff have been threatened at knifepoint. In a number of London schools, teachers have even hired private security firms with sniffer dogs to check pupils for drugs to try and stem the county lines phenomenon.

In June 2019, rival gangs of schoolboy gangsters in south London attacked each other with knives as terrified teachers and other pupils ran to take cover.

It seems that even when London's street gangsters retreat to a neutral location of their choice, trouble is also sure to follow.

THE BARBER SHOP

In *Top Boy* series one, Dushane and Sully wait for an intended murder victim to come out of a barber's shop close to the fictional Summerland Estate. That barber shop is the epicentre of the daytime social scene on the estate. It's been very much like this in the real street gang world for many decades.

In October 2019, two men and three teenage boys went on trial accused of murdering a rival gang member in a north London barber's. Kamali Gabbidon-Lynck, nineteen, bled to death in front of customers, including children. One of the teenage defendants who stood trial for the killing was later stabbed in prison because he'd given an account to police, albeit very limited, of what happened that night.

Barber shops are part of an especially long tradition when it comes to London's Caribbean residents, who flocked to the UK capital in the 1950s and 1960s. Sometimes these barbers open exclusively for gangsters at certain times of the day, although none of the staff would ever actually admit they do this.

One former street gangster explained: "The barbers themselves are usually quiet characters. They don't say much but they hear a lot. When I was in a crew, at least six of us would go in together and take over the shop, so no strangers could come in while we was getting our hair cut."

And there are certain rules inside such barber shops, too. No drugs to be sold or used and most of the customers are encouraged to stay off their phones, in case the barbers hear more than is healthy for them.

T-Bone is a typical barber. He's originally from Barbados in the Caribbean. His shop is located right on the edge of one of London's most notorious housing estates.

"Business is good because everyone come here and they know that anything they talk about here will not go beyond these four walls," explained T-Bone.

He claims he was once in a street gang but was allowed to leave on condition he set up a barber shop near the estate. Street gangsters even helped finance the business. T-Bone explained: "The deal was that they could come here anytime they wanted and I'd make sure there was no strangers in at the same time as them."

T-Bone insisted there had not been any violent incidents involving gangsters since he opened in 2016. He explained:

"I think these crews look on this place as sacred. After all, it's a neutral venue."

One of the few things T-Bone admits discussing with his most important customers is *Top Boy*. He explained: "We all like it. Sure, it's a bit over the top at times but it's got the rhythm right and the characters are just like some of the bluds who come in here."

POSHIES

The UK capital's drug consumption does not just revolve around crackheads and junkies on street corners. There is a potent, wealthy middle class throughout London whose thirst for drugs has helped make many real top boys and their food suppliers extremely wealthy.

Until twenty years ago, this lucrative marketplace was out of bounds to most street gangsters, especially those operating from sprawling council estates. Back then middlemen – often white – dealt with these customers, who were keen to avoid direct contact with real criminals.

But these days street gangsters have their own specific crew members selected to deal directly with the "poshies", as they're known.

These type of wealthy citizens claim that they are occasional recreational users of drugs and infer that somehow excuses them from responsibility for the misery and poverty connected to all sides of the narcotics business.

One former Scotland Yard drug squad officer explained: "The middle-class dinner-party guests of London don't like facing the uncomfortable truth that many of them are helping prop up the capital's drugs trade and all the misery associated with that. That includes taking some responsibility for the knife epidemic as well."

One west London street gangster explained: "Supplying food to middle-class people in their safe, secure designer homes is a lot more risky than selling £5 wraps of dubs on a council estate.

"Junkies never dare confront you. They simply pay their money and disappear.

"But it's different with middle-class users. They expect you to deliver food to their posh homes, come in for a drink like some sort of circus act while all their mates go, 'Ooh that's a drug dealer criminal. How daring and exciting'.

"But that's when a dealer is at his or her most vulnerable. You don't know who half the fuckin' people are at that dinner party. They might be coppers for all you know and you can be sure someone will blabber about you to outsiders."

Another former street gangster explained: "I had these smart alec type poshie customers who'd bleat about whether I'd sold them a full gram or if the stuff had been watered down too much. That's not how you're supposed to talk to someone in my game.

"You either hand over the money for the food or you stay the fuck away from this 'world'. A lot of these middle-class types don't get it. But I have to keep my trap shut even when they're mouthing off at me, because I can't afford to upset them, in case they grass me up to the feds."

Current Metropolitan Police Commissioner Cressida Dick has accused middle-class London drug users of helping fuel the ultra-violent world of street gangs.

She said: "There are groups of middle-class people who sit round happily thinking about global warming and fair trade and environmental protection and all sorts of things, organic food, but think there's no harm in taking a bit of cocaine. Well, there is. There is misery throughout the supply chain."

ROBBIN' HOOD

Towards the end of *Top Boy* series one, young Summerhouse Estate schoolboy Ra'Nell's mum discovers that her young son has been beaten up by a drug dealer, so she turns to crime boss Dushane to punish her son's attacker. Dushane shows another side to his character by going round to sort out the dealer.

It's a pivotal scene because it provides an insight into how top boys like Dushane sometimes happily provide Robin Hood-type services to maintain a hold over the estate where they work and live.

In the real world of top boys, street gangs have been hailed by some residents as the saviours of the housing estates where they live and operate.

One former street gang member explained: "There is another side to the gang world inside those estates. It's not just about shooting and sticking a blade in your rivals and selling wraps of food to junkies.

"A good top boy knows only too well that keeping the residents happy and content is vital to avoid any problems. Sure, most are too scared to ever go to the feds about us. But we also try to put something back into the community as well, because that then makes our jobs easier."

It's been claimed recently that there are even street gangsters providing shopping delivery services to elderly residents, who're too ill to venture out.

"Obviously they have an ulterior motive," explained another former street gangster. "A good top boy likes to keep the old 'uns in their flats because he doesn't want too many being vacated, otherwise that can lead to new residents moving in who might be feds or troublemakers from rival gangs."

The key to any street gang operation is to control all elements of their housing estate. One gangster explained: "We like to run everything that goes in and out of our estate, even down to who gets to live in any empty flats."

Other Robin Hood-style activities on these crime-riddled estates include crews cleaning corridors and the inside of elevators. The same gang member explained: "The idea is to make the residents feel grateful to us, then we know they'll always be on our side.

"Also, it belittles the local authority who're supposed to be doing those jobs themselves. We're telling them to keep away because we're in charge and a lot of the time they really do just back off.

"Who'd want to go into an estate and be threatened for trying to do some cleaning? Much easier to let the 'locals' do it themselves, eh?"

STREET JUSTICE

It's claimed that street gangs "police" many of the most notorious estates across London and hand out severe punishments to any resident who breaks their rules.

One former gang member explained: "One time we was told that an old guy was luring kids into his flat to abuse them. Some of the parents came to us after the police failed to arrest this old man.

"We launched our own investigation and established this old guy was definitely a paedo. So we went round to his flat and carved him up. He was hurt bad but refused to go to hospital because he was convinced we'd take over his flat while he was gone."

The following day, the gang got a call from a resident to say the same old man had jumped off his balcony.

The former gangster explained: "No one knew if he did it himself or was thrown."

Three gangsters rapidly removed the man's corpse from the roof of a car he'd landed on. Then they "disposed of it" before anyone asked awkward questions so they could then move into his flat. They paid the old man's rent as if he was still alive.

The same former soldier explained: "It was a cool location because you could see all the entrances and exits to most of the estate from its windows. We turned it into a food factory for months until the feds started asking questions and then we moved out."

JAMMIN'

Top Boy gives the clear impression that many street gangs have a "live today, gone tomorrow" attitude built around splashing their p's out on fast cars, women and designer trainers.

This attitude pervades throughout much of the TV series and it adds an understandable sense of edginess and glamour to a lot of the action.

In the real world it's much the same story; there are few street gangsters who actually save their ill-gotten gains and end up retiring and living happily ever after.

Original top boy Gordy is a rare exception to that rule. Now in his mid-forties, he left his London street gang and rebooted his life running a gym inside the same west London gang territory he ruled with a rod of iron twenty years ago.

But he knows only too well that being out of the street gang world does not guarantee him safety.

Gordy explained: "I left the streets because another crew was taking over my territory. Instead of fighting back I started afresh and I'm alive today because of that decision."

Gordy's gym membership even includes some former street gangsters. In some ways he's similar to trainer Leon in series one of *Top Boy*, who sees himself as someone who can help kids avoid the pitfalls he experienced.

Gordy offer youths an alternative to the gang life by encouraging fitness and interest in specific sports ranging from football to boxing. He claims he's helped turned around the lives of many troubled youths on the verge of joining street gangs in west London.

Gordy hates the gangs in his neighbourhood because he knows only too well that they are such an integral part of the world they all live in. He knows they still lure kids in to their web of crime and then use them until they don't need them any more.

Gordy explained: "I don't always succeed with keeping kids out of gangs. It's hard because some of them have nowhere else to turn. I see the potential in most kids but they have to turn their backs on a gang specifically, otherwise they'll end up in one. What a waste of their life."

Gyms like the one which Gordy runs provide an outlet for the aggression that so often dominates London's real streets. Rigorous training also helps those hooked on drugs to find an alternative to their long-term dependence. Exercise also undoubtedly helps with people's mood swings. Many say it "sweats those bad feelings away" and it's true.

But Gordy admitted: "Training can't solve all problems. These kids have to make up their own minds ultimately. That's the challenge."

It's hard to resist the temptation when membership of a street gang brings with it protection from outside violence and interference. So life goes round and round on London's notorious street gang-run estates, providing an endless cycle of misery and deprivation that helps feed endless material into the *Top Boy* TV franchise.

But what are the secret ingredients which have helped this show become such a must-watch series for so many?

ACT 3
TV'S TOP BOY

This is England where you can
be a villain or a victim.

KANO

THE CREATOR AND
HIS MASTERPLAN

Shouts and threats could clearly be heard from a corridor next to the A&E department reception area. Two groups of angry youths were screaming into each other's faces. They pushed and shoved each other while visitors and staff tried to stay out of their way.

The confrontation was disorganised and random and a few punches were thrown. Outside the hospital, a shirtless young man hooked up to a drip with blood-soaked dressings on wounds on his arms and shoulder traded shoves with another youth.

Television script writer Ronan Bennett witnessed all this as he left hospital where his daughter had just been born. It had a profound effect on him. Then came an incident close to his home in Hackney that further fuelled what would eventually become the concept for TV's *Top Boy*.

Bennett was at his local supermarket when he noticed a twelve-year-old boy hanging around in the forecourt. A man in his mid-twenties approached the boy and exchanged a few words. The kid then slipped off to a nearby alley between a burger bar and a second-hand furniture shop.

The man drew on a cigarette while looking up and down the street as he waited. Then the child reappeared. The pair did a street handshake. The kid then spat on the ground and walked off. The man then casually stooped to retrieve something on the ground and went on his way.

A few weeks later Ronan Bennett saw the boy again and approached him. He assured him he was not a fed but their conversation ended quickly when the boy said Bennett would have to pay him for loss of business, unless he left immediately.

Bennett was later told by a senior police officer that as long as there were no "ancillary crimes" involved – such as a mugging or a burglary – then that child wouldn't be arrested. Bennett then came across a youth on the streets near his home who claimed he'd first held a gun when he was nine or ten.

The same youth said he stored a revolver at his family's flat for an estate crew of street gangsters headed by a ruthless top boy. The youth later claimed he was paid thousands to keep the weapon hidden under his bed. It was much more likely he received a fiver for his troubles.

This youth also revealed to writer Bennett that he did his first drug deal aged twelve with food provided by his own father, who ordered his son to catch a cab and take a package of drugs to an address outside London. The youth handed over the parcel in exchange for an envelope full of cash.

Ronan Bennett also kept noticing all the police stop and search incidents on the streets near his east London home. He heard about violent street gang attacks, fingers cut off, a man buried alive, another tortured with an iron. Bennett recorded many interviews with real people to make sure he got their voices right. Then he checked with locals to ensure his ideas were feasible and realistic.

The characters we now watch on *Top Boy* are a figment of Bennett's vivid imagination but they're also extremely reflective of what can happen on a feral housing estate in an urban environment.

While Bennett has lived in Hackney for many years, he was actually brought up in Northern Ireland. This no doubt explains his affinity with the disaffected youths who're vital to the *Top Boy* TV series. Bennett's pleasant Hackney home on a nice, tree-lined street is only a few hundred yards from the frontline that borders the type of housing estate so typified by his *Top Boy* creation, Summerhouse.

SERIES ONE

The history of *Top Boy* is a perfect reflection of the way that the threat of street gangs at the start of the last decade had been ignored for many years because it was considered a "black problem" by London's police.

The first series was originally pitched to the BBC as a one-off TV film. The corporation balked at the language and its stark gang-related subject matter, which their mainly white executives struggled to relate to. So creator Ronan Bennett took it to Channel 4, who commissioned it.

Top Boy's first season – broadcast over four consecutive nights, from 31 October to 3 November 2011 – was an instant hit. The audience believed they were watching something authentic and reacted with great excitement and praise.

But then some of those younger viewers discovered that *Top Boy* had been created by a white middle-aged Irishman. How could he possibly understand the gritty inner-city chaos so well portrayed on *Top Boy*?

"He knows what it's like on the streets whether it's east London or Belfast, it boils down to the same thing," one *Top Boy* crew member later commented.

Actor Ashley Walters – who plays top boy Dushane – agreed: "Ronan lives in the heart of the show, and he has seen these things happen, and it's what made him want to write it."

Ronan Bennett himself told one reporter: "*Top Boy*'s about character, the creation of a world. The aim of the makers is to take viewers viscerally and emotionally to a place they have heard a lot about but don't really know. There's a lot of bad in that world, but also a lot of good, and it's just around the corner, a hundred metres up the road."

Top Boy's first series won a Royal Television Society award for best drama and musical genius Brian Eno won a BAFTA for his score.

SEASON TWO

The second season of *Top Boy* was a remarkable insight into creator Ronan Bennett's strength of character because his wife, journalist Georgina Henry, was suffering from sinus cancer at the time he was writing it.

He'd take her to hospital for tests, scans and consultations with specialists, while trying to also snatch some time on his laptop. Bennett's producers understandably feared he might not be able to complete the scripts for the new series.

At home, Bennett had become the main parent looking after two young children. He later said he poured all the emotion, helplessness and turmoil he felt about his wife's fate into the *Top Boy* series two storylines.

He even featured some emotive hospital scenes, which were no doubt a direct result of the many visits connected to his wife's illness. There was a darkness to series two with death hanging over many of the characters.

Bennett later admitted that he could have written a more upbeat ending for series two if his head had been in a different place. Series one had left viewers with a sense of hope but season two closed with the death of a child and Dushane running for his life.

As Bennett himself later explained: "There was no hope because at the time I was living without hope."

The second series of *Top Boy* aired over four consecutive nights on Channel 4 from 20 August 2013 and it was just as enthusiastically received as series one. Channel 4 immediately ordered a pilot script to be written for a third season.

Then they suddenly pulled the plug and cancelled the show after some executives at the channel decided the drama should be axed because they didn't believe it could further expand its audience. Many were disappointed because *Top Boy* had managed to expose the reality of London street gangs to an audience of whom many didn't even know the gangs existed until the show was screened.

Dushane actor Ashley was bitterly disappointed when the original *Top Boy* was cancelled. But initially he tried to be pragmatic about it and told one interviewer at the time: "As an actor you pull your socks up and look for the next job."

But within days of the series being cancelled, Ashley's social media account "started to go crazy for it". Every day at least fifty messages appeared online demanding the show come back.

So Ashley himself tried to drum up support for a new series but, as he later admitted, he got nowhere fast.

As a result, creator Ronan Bennett and his producers and cast moved on to other things. Then some time later, one particularly avid fan of the series appeared on the horizon and offered *Top Boy* a lifeline.

SEASON THREE

Canadian rap star Drake – real name Aubrey Drake Graham – is a man of many talents: singer, songwriter, producer, actor and businessman. He was born in Toronto on 24 October 1986.

Drake had become an avid fan of the first two series of *Top Boy* after being recommended it while on tour. He liked it so much, he posted stills from the show on Instagram and made a few clumsy attempts at replicating the London slang on social media.

Drake was mystified that Channel 4 had cancelled the series, especially after he heard that TV executives had ordered a new pilot script to be written just after series two was aired.

The rap star made contact with Ashley Walters and they talked about how the show could be resurrected.

Drake revealed to Ashley his own troubled childhood, which he believed had made him able to relate so closely to *Top Boy*. His parents divorced when he was five years old. He and his mother remained in Toronto, while his father returned to Memphis, where he was imprisoned for a number of years on drug charges.

Around this time Drake founded the OVO Sound record label with long-time collaborator 40 and they immediately put even more *Top Boy* references on social media accounts. But none of this persuaded Channel 4 to change its mind. *Top Boy* looked, as they say in the trade, to be dead in the water.

Meanwhile, Drake had become one of the world's bestselling music artists, with over 150 million records sold. He was ranked as the world's highest-certified digital singles artist by the Recording Industry Association of America. He also had the most charted songs – more than 200 – among solo artists in the history of the *Billboard* Hot 100. There were also multiple GRAMMYs and many other prestigious awards.

But none of this counted for much in the world of TV production as Drake's plan to resurrect *Top Boy* continued to hit the buffers.

Then, in 2017 – three years after last talking to Ashley Walters – Drake contacted the producers of *Top Boy* and asked to meet them with writer/creator Ronan Bennett. Drake and his manager-partner, Future, emphasised to the *Top Boy* team how much they still loved the show and its music and wanted to try and help get it up and running again.

An agreement was made to approach Netflix and Drake attended a pitch meeting with the streaming giant's executives. He told them that the series showed a world that was ignored. Young people – white and black and everything in between – identified with it.

Top Boy, Drake said, would introduce a new world to many viewers. That's why it was in many ways better suited to the global streaming "stage" than as the more localised TV drama it had been when Channel 4 produced the first two series.

Within an hour of the meeting, Netflix ordered a new season, with both Ashley Walters and Kane Robinson reprising their roles. Series creator Ronan Bennett returned to script most episodes, along with the original creative team, plus Drake and some of his team joining the series as executive producers.

But this time there would be ten meaty episodes rather than the previous two four-part series. The increased number of episodes would help give the characters and the plotlines more texture and depth.

The show was to be located in London in 2019 and include topical references from immigration laws to the youth violence epidemic. Since the end of series two, chilling county lines operations had become synonymous with the type of street gangs featured in *Top Boy*.

Original *Top Boy* creator Ronan Bennett's job was to further develop the characters in the new longer format series to cope with the exposure of those ten full-length Netflix episodes. Also, the new series would have to accurately reflect how the characters had got older (although no wiser).

For example, Sully's friendship with young street orphan Jason would evolve into a father/son thing, which would greatly help the audience uncover Sully's more "humane" side.

But first of all, the cast needed to sit down and reconnect after years away from *Top Boy*.

READ-THROUGH

By the middle of 2018, the total number of offences in London involving a knife had risen to a seven-year high of 40,147. There were 1,299 stabbings in the capital in the first four months of that year.

It was in the middle of this street crime meltdown – just a few months after Drake had helped secure the Netflix commission – that the *Top Boy* cast assembled for a read-through of the third series scripts at an office in London.

All those present that day talked about the skyrocketing problems out on the capital's real streets to rap star Drake as they went through the episodes. Drake made a point of reassuring actor/rapper Kano – who plays Sully – and the rest of the cast that he would never change any aspect of the series. He just wanted to support it back on to the small screen as a genuine fan.

During that first read-through, it soon became clear that the actors' lines would carry even more meaning and nuance. Not only was it the key to the show's ever-increasing sense of authenticity, but many present that day had experienced first hand the damage being inflicted by London's street gangs.

"There was an edge to that read-through," one member of the show's production staff later explained. "The actors felt it was their duty to use their dialogue to expose what was happening out there on the real streets."

A classic example was when the script called for top boy Sully to order someone to be killed. In the original script his character simply said: "Kill him."

Kano – who plays Sully – saw it differently and changed that line during the read-through to: "Light him up."

The difference in emphasis was there for all to see. Those three words changed everything for the audience and perfectly summed up the little touches that go into making such a collaborative project.

The actors at that read-through all agreed that the key to series three was that it should have more of a social conscience. The show would share issues with its audience. There were many subjects which needed to be put out there.

The cast and producers conversed about how Summerhouse Estate kid Stefan's African-born mother – who's lived in the UK for eighteen years – is arrested by immigration officers and told she'll be thrown out of the country because her papers are not in order.

The cast wanted to ensure their audience would actually see and appreciate why these characters were making certain decisions, many of which were highly relevant to the real problems on London's streets. This would also further humanise these gangsters, which in turn ensured that an even larger audience related to them.

It was just one of many examples of how *Top Boy* had its finger on the pulse of street gangsterdom, without slowing down the dramatic pace of the series.

Other subjects would also be expertly slotted into the new third series, including the Windrush deportation scandal and even the omnipresent modern-day London urban threat of acid attacks.

One former street gangster explained: "This is the type of shit that happens to people like us on estates every day of our lives. They're often the reason why so many people get desperate and go bad. You get pulled into temptation not by choice but by circumstance."

Dushane and Sully were now in their mid-thirties, complete with bigger bellies, but their goals and problems were ongoing and still boiled down to money and power in that order.

When series one had aired back in 2011, knife crime was still in its relative infancy. Some even believed that this worked against the success of the series back then because many feds refused to recognise that the problem of armed street gangsters could escalate as it did.

Others wrongly claimed that *Top Boy*'s first two series glamorised the use of weapons by youths and that this helped fuel the knife epidemic sweeping through London and many of the UK's biggest cities.

"The truth is that all the signs were there way before *Top Boy*'s first series was even created," explained one former south London street gangster.

"Fear is what drives youths to arm themselves. They don't set out to target specific rivals. They're just terrified that they will be killed if they don't make sure they hit back first."

Creator Ronan Bennett and the actors believed they had a responsibility to show how London had gone backwards in terms of knife crime and drugs over the previous six years since the second Channel 4 series was aired.

Sadly, that gap between the end of series two and the start of series three provided many uncomfortable truths when it came to the increasingly deadly streets of London and many other UK cities.

MOVING WITH THE TIMES

As the *Top Boy* franchise reopened for business in 2018, the wholesale gentrification of the area of Hackney where *Top Boy*'s fictional Summerhouse Estate was located continued. The demographics of the area had altered even more since the first two *Top Boy* series at the start of the last decade.

This meant that a lot of the borough's poorer residents had been pushed out of their homes to enable so-called fat-cat developers to buy up estates and turn them into blocks of private luxury flats.

At the time, London's Southwark Council was in the process of selling one vast housing estate – which had been completed in 1974 – for £50 million, having spent £44 million moving most of the three thousand residents out.

This mirrored the *Top Boy* series three plotline, during which Dushane found himself caught up with a group of greedy property developers planning to buy off the Summerhouse Estate.

Many locals would be kicked out of their homes to make way for this new development. They'd be placed in other properties around the country, often within communities they knew nothing about.

New faces would also be vital to the freshness of *Top Boy*'s new Netflix format. Returning to the small screen after such a long absence is fairly unprecedented in TV history. Dushane and Sully's crew at Summerhouse needed to reflect exactly that timespan on the small screen.

As one fan explained: "*Top Boy* needed to move with the times. That was the key to its longevity. The new stories would weave in and out of the old but neither should hold back the other, if you know what I mean."

The show's casting director Des Hamilton also had personal experience of the *Top Boy* environment. This no doubt gave him even more empathy towards the tragic real-life versions of these characters. He was highly instrumental in helping to unlock the potential of many debut cast members. Des had assembled the original first and second series cast and would do the same for all subsequent Netflix "editions" of *Top Boy*.

The storylines that the actors covered during that first read-through with Drake turned out to be even more gripping than in the previous two series. And when the show was eventually filmed and then aired in private screenings, test audience ratings went through the roof. Not surprisingly, a fourth series was commissioned before series three had even been aired.

The new series of *Top Boy* finally premiered on Netflix on 13 September 2019. It was billed as season one, whilst the original two shorter Channel 4 series were billed as *Top Boy: Summerhouse*.

Not only was this drama gripping for an audience but it was performed by many who'd never even acted before. However, they brought with them particular skill sets direct from the street.

CROSSOVER

Many of *Top Boy*'s stars share a background in music. But then rappers across the globe have featured in movies and TV series for more than a quarter of a century, especially in Hollywood.

Films from the 1990s such as *Boyz in the Hood*, *Menace to Society* and *Poetic Justice* featured breakout roles for rappers. Then came the middle-of-the-road movie *Friday*, starring former NWA member Ice Cube. It cost about four million dollars to make and ended up grossing thirty million dollars.

Some consider rapping to be a form of acting. Certainly many of those performers can make you laugh and cry with their music, and they could do the same through acting. Ultimately, where you come from, how hard you spit your lyrics and how much they mean seems to translate into acting. These performers had roles that were authentic to their own experiences – and audiences' expectations. That made them even less of a risk for producers and directors, with the added bonus of bringing with them a built-in fanbase from their music.

And the music that many of these artists personified would become part of *Top Boy*'s lifeblood.

RYTHYM OF LIFE

Music is often the common denominator that links the lives of many London street gangs. The violent nature of some of those sounds seems to add an edge to this chilling netherworld.

But the challenge for the makers of *Top Boy* has always been to find a balance between the so-called real street music and the sounds that would help this drama through all its highs and lows. These sounds also provide the series with atmosphere and street cred as well as helping audiences relate more closely to the characters and their predicaments.

As a result, *Top Boy* has a special kind of synergy. The large sales of many tracks featured on the series prove this point even more emphatically.

One fan explained: "I've got all the music from *Top Boy*. I like playing it on my headphones as I walk around the streets. It makes me more alert to the sort of stuff that *Top Boy* warns you about. It's like the rhythm of life. It helps me survive."

Despite Netflix's global brand now being firmly attached to the show, the series's original composer Brian Eno's subtle background tracks continue to evolve to this day. The former Roxy Music veteran is lauded as one of film and television's finest and most innovative composers.

And while Eno undoubtedly laid the groundwork, rappers from many eras and nations have had their sounds scattered throughout *Top Boy*.

A classic example is UK hip hop veteran Roots Manuva. His track "Fighting For?" contains poignant lines that sum up the netherworld of these feckless young gangsters.

Blood may well be thicker than water
But war will arrive with no word of warning

Another standout track is Ghostpoet's "Cold Win", used in series two. Its atmospheric sound combined with moving, highly relevant rap lyrics provide a perfect musical backdrop to the Summerhouse Estate.

Saving up the pennies cos the city's too gritty
And cooking french fries ain't pretty

So with *Top Boy* set to run for many more seasons, the UK's lively rap scene thrives alongside it. This means a lot of new talent has emerged from the very same inner-city streets where the series is located.

STREET SOUNDS

Grime and drill have evolved during the same era that has seen the rise of *Top Boy*.

Grime tends to be fast-paced and quite punchy while drill is often slower and relies more on melodies. But they're similar, and their core audiences often stand alongside each other.

Back in 2004, UK rapper Nasty Jack named his new version of London rap grime because he'd created it on a grimy estate in Bow, east London, similar in many ways to the Summerhouse Estate featured in *Top Boy*.

Drill, meanwhile, originated on the gritty streets of Chicago, although a version evolved in London just after grime appeared. Drill is also referred to as trap, which was originally another US subgenre of hip hop during the late 1990s. Trap is gangster slang for a flat or house taken over to sell and package drugs from.

UK trap and drill have certainly attracted a more "feral" crowd. Some have accused drill and trap of deliberately appealing more to real street gangsters. But others rightly point out that music alone cannot be held responsible in any way for encouraging London's young to turn to crime.

Certainly many tracks have unashamedly in the recent past used violence and crime as a lyrical backdrop. And while grime and drill have developed international brands of rap alongside each other, their MCs can be highly competitive with each other.

Grime and drill fans often watch their favourite MCs competing against each other on stage in what's known as "clashing". Most of the time these concerts are trouble-free but there have been flare-ups caused mainly by the real street gangster fans especially attracted to drill.

Standout grime and drill rappers also take great care not to look down at their audiences. UK drill crew 67 is a classic example. Their main rappers include Scribz, Dimzy, Monkey, ASAP and Liquez.

These MCs speak *to* people, not *at* them. It is this connection to the audience that is the driving force behind London's unique brands of rap.

In much the same way, *Top Boy* also prides itself on not talking down to its audience by operating on a level that everyone in the audience can relate to.

One drill fan explained: "Drill and trap are the same in essence. They unashamedly appeal to young gangsters and disaffected youths out there on the street having to commit crimes to survive."

As a result, mainstream media in the UK have alleged that some of *Top Boy*'s musical tracks have direct links to real-life gang "problems" in the UK.

"That's no big deal," said one ex-west London gang member. "Making it big in drill appeals to real gangsters because they're the ones often being written about in these rappers' songs."

Being a real gangster doesn't gain you entry into the music business but it doesn't stop you attending clashes, either.

That seems to come with the territory.

THE IN-CROWD

A lot of real street gangsters see themselves as stars of rap songs that tell the story of London's drugs underworld.

Rapper Kano – who stars as top boy Sully – says the truth behind these songs is what makes them so popular. And Kano's raps undoubtedly come from his own first-hand experiences. He explained: "The difference in music is the control, whereas doing this [acting], it's someone else's words that you can play in your own way."

Actor Ashley Thomas – also known as Bashy – strikes a clever balance with his portrayal of Jermaine in *Top Boy*. As a music artist, Thomas has also worked closely as a producer with Tinie Tempah, Wretch 32, Chipmunk and Big Narstie.

Also in the background musical mix for *Top Boy* are talented artists ranging from Nolay to Ghetts to President T, plus Devil Man from Birmingham. All this talent has thrived, thanks to *Top Boy*'s huge global audience.

And to add to the show's street music credentials it's worth noting that *Top Boy* star Ashley Walters and London hip hop vet Roots Manuva both attended the same music course at Pimlico School in Central London.

The musical content in *Top Boy* has also convinced many fans that they "own" the series in a sense. They expect their favourite characters to behave in a certain manner and that enables them to accept their extreme behaviour as a result.

This in turn helps audiences engage with everything they're watching. But it can blur the lines between the imaginary world of series creator Ronan Bennett and the brutal real top boys and their crews, whose crimes have dominated London's underworld for at least the last ten years.

One *Top Boy* fan explained: "When you watch *Top Boy* you don't think, oh, that's actor Ashley Walters out there, you believe he *is* the *Top Boy*. He is that person, warts and all. That is what good TV drama should be about."

Meanwhile, over in real east London, there is one place above all else where many connected to grime and drill gather.

WESTFIELD

The Westfield Shopping Centre in Stratford has long been popular with residents from many of east London's most notorious housing estates. It's also been at the centre of some nasty street gang clashes in recent years.

Unfortunately, Westfield is a natural hub for these sorts of characters, containing obligatory designer stores and multiple fast food outlets.

It's the type of place where real top boys do their Christmas shopping: a vast subterranean retail version of the concrete jungle housing estates that so many street gangsters hail from.

As one grime artist rapped:

Go inside the one [Westfield] in east London to see the top boys out buying gold and diamonds for their girls.

KEEPING IT REAL

Would *Top Boy* be as successful (or watchable) without the current cast? One fan explained: "That's a tricky one to answer because we know and love them thanks to characters written by the show's creator. It's hard to know if we'd feel the same way if different actors were playing those roles."

Top Boy's ultimate partners-in-crime, Dushane and Sully, expose a world of twisted power struggles. Audiences often overlook the coldly rational and ruthless decision-making of a bunch of territorial gangsters in a modern urban landscape.

But then many *Top Boy* performers come from the very same streets and housing estates that this drama is centred around. They know all about the real dangers that exist within these communities. And this undoubtedly helps the actors perform even more convincingly for *Top Boy* fans.

But where did the show's characters and the actors who play them come from? And how have their backgrounds helped them turn *Top Boy* into a brilliant exposé of London's street gangs?

TOP BOY'S CHARACTERS

DUSHANE

Ashley Walters – who plays Dushane – knows all about real-life guns and crime. Back in 2002 – when he was a teenage singer with London rap outfit So Solid Crew – he was found in possession of a gun and bullets after being stopped in his car by the feds.

Ashley subsequently appeared at Southwark Crown Court, where he pleaded guilty to having a loaded firearm. He was given eighteen months in a young offenders' institution for possessing the weapon.

He later explained: "I had an inkling that I was going to prison before I actually did, because I'd witnessed my father and my elders going through it. It seemed like that's the way that you got respect, which is a sad thing. But that indoctrinated mind still exists in those areas."

Today, Ashley insists prison taught him to be "smarter" about how he lives and who he spends time with and left him "ready to take on the world but in a different way".

But he also doesn't regret the mistakes he's made in the past. He explained: "It's made me the person I am today.

If I hadn't had my jail experience, if I hadn't had the negative experiences with So Solid, would I be credible enough to play Dushane? Who knows? You have to take the rough with the smooth."

Ashley also claimed he was carrying that gun for his own protection because "a lot of people were rolling around with guns". But Ashley conceded that the feds had a right to stop him "and they weren't wrong".

However, Ashley condemned the police for generally stopping people "just because of the colour of their skin". Until he joined *Top Boy* in 2011, Ashley reckoned he'd been stopped and searched on average at least three times a month.

Ashley Walters' commitment to *Top Boy* from the get-go undoubtedly helped the programme get commissioned by Channel 4 in the first place. Today, he's a relatively seasoned veteran actor, but he was clearly a much rawer talent when *Top Boy*'s first season emerged in 2011.

A few years earlier, Ashley starred in *Bullet Boy*, long considered a movie that set the tone for the *Top Boy* franchise. In that film, Ashley played eighteen-year-old Ricky, fresh out of jail. He and his twelve-year-old brother, Curtis, struggle to survive when a minor street clash escalates into an all-out neighbourhood war.

Bullet Boy broke a lot of the usual "rules" when it comes to so-called urban dramas. The film marked out its territory and found an audience who wanted to be immersed in such a dangerous but relatable criminal netherworld, which revolved around a London housing estate.

Ashley Walters' character Ricky in *Bullet Boy* tries to escape the murder and mayhem of his local manor but he never makes it.

Back to *Top Boy*: Dushane speaks with a distinct east London street accent in the series, even though actor Ashley Walters is actually from Peckham, in south London.

In one scene, street soldier Dris provides a cache of rusty old firearms for boss Dushane and their posse to use to hijack a rival gang and steal their drugs.

"Where d'you get these, bruv?" Dushane asks Dris. "Antique roadshow?"

Then Dushane notices a sawn-off shotgun in the bottom of the arms cache bag, pulls it out and says: "Hmmm. This is a bit better."

That snub-nosed lethal weapon represents a throwback to the bad old days of the old-school British blaggers of the 1970s and 1980. Those robbers were the heroes of their hoods back then and their favourite weapon was the sawn-off.

On *Top Boy*'s fictional Summerhouse Estate, gangster Dushane dreams of making enough p's to get out of the drugs game while business partner Sully seems addicted to it all in series one. Dushane is street-smart and ambitious and much less impulsive than Sully but he evolves into the coldly ambitious one. Ashley Walters has admitted that he himself made many other mistakes during his teens and he still has a lot of friends who work on estates as top boys or soldiers.

In *Top Boy*, Dushane reaches the top of his game only to discover that now he's made it, everyone wants to knock him off his perch because there's always someone ready to take his crown.

TOP BOY P'S

The p's – money – are the driving motivation for the street gangsters headed up by top boy Dushane, who tries to hire all his new recruits with the promise of cash.

Ashley Walters concedes he himself was "dazzled by money" growing up and "lost a lot of money" after signing his first record deal with no legal representation.

Top Boy fans find Dushane's character highly relatable because he seems more reflective than most street gangsters. He's also methodical about his "business". It's almost as if he's playing a game of chess.

Dushane has grown up on the Summerhouse Estate and feels he has no option but to sell drugs. He still lives with mother, Pat, a devout churchgoer, but is determined to hold onto his top boy crown.

In real life, Ashley Walters was brought up on an estate similar to the fictional Summerhouse and, just like Dushane, he also has a strong mum. But unlike Dushane, Ashley credits his mother with helping to save him from a life of crime.

Ashley told one reporter: "She's a very strong mum. She always kept her eye on me and never let me get involved in any of that stuff."

Ashley shares many other character traits with Dushane. He had his first child as a teenager. Although today he insists he was always determined not to repeat his own father's mistakes.

For as much as Ashley wanted to hang out with friends, there was usually someone on his back pushing him in the right direction.

Ashley explained: "They always told me what the right thing to do was, and what was the wrong thing to do. I also always had extra responsibility because I had kids – you can't be there for your kids in a prison cell."

But Ashley admitted he doesn't work to a rule book when it comes to bringing up the eight kids he now has. He had three children with his first partner. Two more followed with another partner, who lives in Leeds.

Ashley and his current actress wife, Danielle Isaie, married in 2013. He is stepfather to his wife's son and has two children from this latest marriage, which he describes as "a traditional set-up". Walters had his eighth child at the age of thirty-four – sixteen years after the birth of his first son, Shayon.

Ashley insists that he's always tried to be a good dad to all his children. He told one reporter recently: "I've grown up being a father. When my first son was born I was seventeen. I was a child bringing up a child. I was not capable of under-standing what a dad was meant to be."

A few years ago, Ashley even presented *Top Dad,* a Channel 4 series featuring fathers in unusual situations. Among them was a reformed gangster, a teenage adoptive father and one undergoing gender reassignment.

Back on *Top Boy* there is always the other "dark side" of Dushane simmering just beneath the surface, thanks to Ashley Walters' powerful acting. After all, Dushane fell off his perch and had to go on his toes to Jamaica at the end of series two when the Albanians came after him in London. This proved that even he was vulnerable.

MAKING WAVES

At the start of series three Dushane is hiding out in Jamaica but he soon quits the island to return to the Summerhouse Estate.

"A leopard doesn't change his spots – ever," Ashley Walters later explained. "Dushane is still a gangster despite laying low in Jamaica and it was only natural that he would want to get back to the city."

Back at Summerhouse, Jamaica-based drug baron Sugar's London rep is making Dushane's life a misery with constant threats, even though Sugar's providing the food for Dushane's gangsters to sell. This is all about pressure and control.

Series three of *Top Boy* is driven by Dushane's relentless determination to retain control of Summerhouse's food business at *any* cost. He also has long term ambitions to supply the rest of the city with food.

Dushane teams up with Sully once again after an earlier fallout because he knows that without Sully he can never achieve his ultimate ambition.

But when Sully opens up about the death of his young friend Jason, Dushane shows complete indifference. It's almost as if he doesn't quite get it. Dushane and Sully seem to be swapping roles.

In series three, Dushane's new girlfriend Shelley enables Dushane to dream about a life beyond the Summerhouse Estate. She wants him to have a normal family and to realise there is more to life than selling drugs.

Ultimately, Dushane may have loads of money and women but he still ends up back home alone with just a large brandy for company.

But what about Dushane's top boy partner in crime, Sully? He's an even more complex and chilling character.

SULLY

There has been a longstanding debate as to whether *Top Boy* glorifies violence. And no character epitomises this more than Sully, portrayed by actor and rapper Kano. Sully provides the audience with a breathtaking insight into a twisted soul by somehow combining genuine heartbreak with out-and-out murderous anger.

Kano puts a lot of his own life experiences and intensity into the part of Sully and tackles the issues head-on. Kano says: "Racism is still everywhere in the UK but it was way worse when my mum turned up in London from Jamaica."

Kano – now in his mid-thirties – was born Kane Brett Robinson in East Ham, east London, with a gift for words and song. He grew up alongside London's grime scene as it developed over the past decade and a half, often among the residents of council estates, including the one where he was brought up.

Kano was an early member of the east London-based N.A.S.T.Y Crew. Then he signed to produce his own solo album, *Home Sweet Home*, in 2005, which featured stand-out tracks including the legendary 'P's And Q's'.

You ain't never weighed the ounce, fought a bouncer
You ain't never hid no blots in your mouth

That track was a watershed moment for Kano as it was viewed more than eight million times on YouTube. This catapulted him from up-and-coming rapper into one of Britain's top MCs.

Meanwhile, his *Top Boy* creation Sully's backstory is that his full name is Gerald Sullivan and he had a Nigerian mother and an Irish father. He's on a brutal "journey" that impacts all the big decisions. Right and wrong are blurred throughout his world and Sully clearly has a death wish.

Sully's impact on the audience is a credit to Kano's skilful acting and some fine writing. It is clear Kano has made the role of Dushane's partner, Sully, his own.

One former south London soldier called Raz told me: "It's all about street cred, bruv. Sully's hard but vulnerable. He's crazy but loving. He's a psycho but he's also a pussy. See what I mean?"

Music artist Kano is himself an intense personality, who thinks deeply about all sorts of issues. He says: "There are so many questions about the country we live in. Questions about the hypocrisy. Questions about our place in this country. Questions about how much we're doing and could we do more, could we care more? Questions about this street thing and how important is that? And how much do you value life?"

In *Top Boy*, Sully and Dushane went to school together, so there is clearly a special bond between them. But Sully is much more hot-headed and rarely thinks things through. One moment he's charming and funny. The next he's turned on a sixpence into a violent, reckless killer.

Hence the pair don't always see eye-to-eye but they keep teaming up over and over again, even after Sully is released from prison. Kano somehow turns this homicidal, psychotic criminal into a loveable character. It's a remarkable achievement.

As Kano himself said recently about his role: "*Top Boy* humanises gangsters. When I play Sully I don't look down at that world because I come from that world. I know why this shit happens."

ROUNDABOUT OF CRIME

In the first two series of *Top Boy*, violence seemed to come too easily to Sully. He was so impulsive that he even kidnapped his own cousin. But by series three Sully is softening as life hits him with blow after blow. Sully even starts questioning the sort of issues which partner Dushane has long since stopped caring about.

In a scene from series three, Sully watches his estranged daughter from a distance outside her school. It's a heartbreaking moment. Sully doesn't really deserve to walk back into her life but he desperately wants to make amends.

Later, when Dushane urges Sully to lighten up and enjoy the p's, Sully admits to his old friend that he doesn't care about the p's any more. Money means nothing to him. Sully has found himself stuck on a roundabout of crime and doesn't know how to get off it. He knows it's wrong but he doesn't know any other life, so what can he do?

When Sully bemoans in *Top Boy* the fact that he spends much of his time sleeping on corner man Dris's sofa, the audience know he's a lonely lost soul with no real sense of purpose.

Television has the power to make audiences sympathise with any character, whether a victim or killer.

One *Top Boy* fan explained: "I really like Sully as a character but I'm not entirely sure why. He's a walking, talking psychopath but you can't help feeling for him a lot of the times."

When Sully and his young friend Jason end up setting off fireworks and having a laugh together on a beach in the seaside town of Ramsgate in Kent, in series three, it's a relief to Sully to be out of the hood, away from Dushane and all the bad things that have haunted his life.

NO ESCAPE

Sully may be lonely but at least he's got that kid Jason to bond with. Sully sees Jason as a version of himself when he was a youngster. Sully's family background emerges through Jason; they both had junkie mothers.

In Ramsgate, a bunch of racist white men try to goad Sully and Jason into a fight as they walk by. Sully holds back uncharacteristically. Maybe he has changed?

But when Sully's young friend Jason dies in a house fire deliberately started by those same racists, it sends Sully on a murderous rampage.

Yet even as he escapes from the blazing building where Jason has just died, Sully still has time to stop and give the immigrants who share the house with them some money to keep them safe.

Sully is emotionally wrecked by the murder of his young friend Jason. He knows he's cracking up. He's clearly no longer the hard-nosed young blud we met in the first two series of *Top Boy*.

But that sense of reflection will be smashed to pieces when Sully decides on revenge and ends up uncontrollably smashing one of the men who started the fire virtually to death with a scaffolding pole.

Afterwards, Sully wades into the sea contemplating suicide. This guy is on the edge of hell. No wonder Kano later admitted he put a lot of emotional energy into his performance.

Kano said: 'It was scary. To play a character with that much depth was hard... But I needed that, it's what an actor dreams of.'

The final couple of episodes of *Top Boy* series three revolve around Dushane and Sully's war against rivals Jamie and Modie. It's back to all-or-nothing stuff, which sums up life in the ghetto for all the anti-heroes of *Top Boy*. For these characters all have one thing in common with the real Top Boys: they're just trying to get through life.

The overriding message from the writers of *Top Boy* is that none of this is worth one death, let alone dozens. Sully knows that in his heart of hearts. But he's in too deep and there is no way out.

JAMIE

In the real world of street gangs, some of the most chilling top boys are under the age of twenty. These characters are often more unpredictable and scary than their older rivals.

So the introduction in series three of Jamie – played by Michael Ward – was essential for the show to continue to be an accurate reflection of the real top boy world.

But Jamie is much more than just a trigger-happy teenage gangster and he very much appealed to *Top Boy*'s audiences across the demographic divide, as well as to men *and* women.

Actor Michael Ward – who portrays Jaimie – lost his dad at a very young age, so he was able to give the role genuine heart and soul. He even closely studied Tommy Shelby in *Peaky Blinders*, Ghost in *Power*, and Denzel Washington in *Training Day* to work out how he was going to play Jamie.

As Michael later explained: "I just wanted to see how they don't really say much, but when they do speak, people listen."

At one stage, Michael's character Jamie even finds himself having to deal with the reality of street gang life when his new girlfriend is shot and killed because of his feud with other street gangsters.

One female fan explained: "*Top Boy*'s not just bang-bang-you're-dead stuff. It goes in real deep on issues through the characters. That makes a lot of it very relatable for women.

"Jamie seems hard as nails on the outside but every now and again he does something soft and thoughtful, which obviously makes him appeal to women in the audience."

Jamie's uniquely soft interpretation of words and dialogue had a profound effect on *Top Boy* series three audiences. A classic example is the way he bumps fists with friends and foes and says, "Bless" or "Respect".

On London's real streets and estates, these two words have evolved from the bad old days of the Yardies. They contain a twisted symbolism, but the way Jamie uses those words in *Top Boy* tells the audience so much about the underlying connection that even the most evil street gangsters have for each other.

"Bless" sounds like a sweet and kindly response that shows you care about someone but in the underworld it also has chilling undertones.

Jamie's use of the word "respect" in *Top Boy* usually involves bigger issues but it tells the audience that these characters try to have some respect for each other at all times, despite any issues between them. If they don't, then that's when problems arise.

One former street gangster explained: "Words like these come from all the suffering of black and other minorities. Remember, black kids don't just turn into gangsters overnight. They often have families who've suffered for generations in a country where black people have not always been welcome."

There's another underlying message connected to Jamie's use of the word "love", too. He only says it when he talks to his two kid brothers, whom he's bringing up singlehandedly and clearly genuinely loves and cares for.

He wants them to know he loves them above all others and that he will never let them down. Or so he hopes.

TWO LIVES

One of the most moving scenes involving Jamie comes when he goes into a hospital with a bunch of flowers to visit an injured girl soldier. He encounters her father and discovers that she'll never fully recover from the attack.

Jamie finds himself having to deal with issues he usually ignores. And the audience are left wondering if he's going to change as a result.

But, inevitably, Jamie ends up remaining a ruthless, hungry ambitious gangster determined to be the top boy, whatever it takes.

He's looking to expand his top boy operations into Summerhouse from a neighbouring estate. This breaks all the territorial rules of the street and he aims to get rid of Dushane and Sully permanently. The type of war has occurred countless time between real London street gangsters.

Jamie's character is a juxtaposition of what happens when events out of your control force you into a life you wouldn't wish on another. And the route to that goal is paved with blood and dead bodies.

Jamie's character also reflects so many real-life single parents. He makes sure his brothers do their homework. He even attends school meetings to find out how they're doing in class.

A lot of the young gangsters I've talked to are adamant that they don't want their siblings to end up like them – even though gangsters so often pay out for their family to survive financially as one unit.

As Jamie says to his two young brothers: "I'm your brother, your mother and your father and don't you forget that."

On one hot summer afternoon, Jamie and his two brothers visit the Old English Garden where the three orphaned brothers gather each year to remember their late parents. It's their mother's birthday and they talk about her, about how strong she was.

Jamie is in tears. The enormity of what he's doing in his "other gangster life" has finally hit him hard. Yet the audience all know that just a few hours earlier he was ordering the execution of a gang rival.

Jamie ends up under attack from all sides. Dushane and Sully are hunting for him and on-the-run former top boy Modie wants back the drugs business he "lent" to Jamie to look after while he was in jail. At the end of series three, Jamie finds himself with no choice but to agree a deal with Dushane in order to stay out of prison and protect his brothers from being dragged into his criminal activities.

In the real world, these dilemmas are not so neatly solved and very few of them have happy endings. But Jamie isn't the only new character in *Top Boy*'s Netflix debut season who captured the audience's undivided attention.

JAQ

Being a drug dealer is all about front. You can't show your fear to anyone. *Top Boy*'s series three girl gangster Jaq is good at impressing this upon all her young bluds, who're manning the corners on the Summerhouse Estate.

When Jaq plays basketball with a bunch of boys on the estate, she seamlessly morphs into one of them. Yet minutes later she is strictly managing another group of estate kids while they sell drugs on her behalf.

Throughout all this, Jaq – played by actress Jasmine Jobson – retains a vulnerable sense of femininity with her peeled back braids. She also happens to be openly gay in a world filled to the brim with blatant, old-fashioned homophobia.

Many have speculated that Jaq is modelled on girl assassin Snoop from the legendary US TV series *The Wire*. There are certain similarities but Jaq remains unique in her own right because of the world she comes from.

Actress Jasmine Jobson's own real-life backstory helps explain a lot of these character traits. She put herself into foster care as a teenager and clearly taps into those experiences for her role as Jaq.

Jasmine is rightly proud of *Top Boy* and insisted that from beginning to end of filming, there was continuous support for herself and all the young series three cast.

She explained: "You know you're going to be a part of something great and special, and then when it actually airs and the public get to see it, their response has been surreal. I can honestly say that I haven't had any negativity from it at all."

Towards the end of series three, an even more complex side to Jaq's character emerges. She discovers her sister had unintentionally told her secret boyfriend, Leighton, about the movements of top boy boss Sully and that information was used to try and kill Sully.

Jaq is so angry she beats her sister up. But in the end, blood does prove thicker than water as she helps her sister flee Dushane and Sully's quest for revenge. They want her dead for ratting on them.

In the real street gangster world these type of clashes occur on virtually a daily basis. An insult or a rumour can quickly lead to an act of murderous revenge from which there is no return.

Back on *Top Boy*, there are many other characters caught up in this television firestorm of crime and violence.

DRIS

On housing estates throughout London, corner men are the unsung "heroes" of the street crews. They are the ones out on the front line pushing the yungers to get sales but at the same time supposedly keeping an eye out for them.

On *Top Boy*'s fictional Summerhouse Estate, corner man Dris – played by Shone Romulus – heads up Dushane's business selling food on the street. Shone was recruited by the series's producers as he hung around the forecourt of a block of flats where he lives in Hackney.

His character Dris is softly spoken and seems vulnerable, especially after it's revealed that he suffered a stroke.

Dris is a single, full-time parent to a young daughter, who represents his other life away from crime. Her mother is serving a long stretch in prison, so Dris has to play mother and father.

He's a kind, loving parent at home with his daughter. Dris even wears spectacles for his short sight. But he could never wear them on the corners because it would ruin his street cred.

Dris's family-man side is a clever ploy by *Top Boy* creator Ronan Bennett to enable the audience to relate more closely to Dris when his life drains away from him as series three progresses. Dris's ongoing health problems even lead to him collapsing while he acts as a lookout while Dushane burgles a house. Dushane coldly accuses Dris of "slacking" and cuts his crew responsibilities even further. It's clear from Dris's face that he knows he is not firing on all cylinders.

Dris's health problems make Dushane and Sully wary of trusting Dris with the big jobs. As a result, Dris seems destined to work the corners for the rest of his life. He's so frozen by his complicated domestic life and health that he seems unable to move forwards or backwards.

"Dris has got issues with everything and everybody," said one big fan of the series. "But he's cool and seems softer than the other street gangsters, which makes him an extremely interesting character."

At the end of series three, Dris faces a bullet from Sully for betraying the top boys. Dris tells Sully: "Everything's fucked. Now do it, fam."

Dris's end is inevitable, like that of so many characters on *Top Boy*. And the message is simple: Crime doesn't pay.

LIZZIE

Jamie's main food supplier, middle-aged blonde Irish drug baroness Lizzie – played by actress Lisa Dwan – debuts in *Top Boy* series three. She even uses an antique shop and the elderly lady who runs it as a front for her drugs empire.

That curiosity shop sums up the divide between her top boy client (and lover) Jamie, and the wealthy, often faceless drug barons who supply the food and then sit back and count the p's without taking any risks themselves.

In the real London underworld, these characters are pulling most of the strings. They're rarely brought to justice, even though they're often the puppet masters who help turned London's underworld into such a deadly place.

In *Top Boy*, Lizzie is both manipulated and manipulative. At times she seems tougher than the top boys she helps to feed but on other occasions she melts down in spectacular style.

However, there is much more to Lizzie than first meets the eye. There are hints that the drug shipments she's selling through Jaimie could be raising cash for disaffected former members of the IRA, who want to re-ignite the Troubles.

Lizzie even lets slip how one of her brothers back in Dublin was murdered during the original Troubles and her other brother was knee-capped. This is not a typical middle-class lady in way too deep.

A lot of this backstory is provided by *Top Boy* creator Ronan Bennett's own experiences in Northern Island. It's used as a device to show the development of Lizzie as a character. Bennett himself was imprisoned in the Long Kesh internment camp in the late 1970s for being a republican activist and there is no doubt this helped him get beneath the skin of the characters he's created for *Top Boy*.

The way Lizzie sleeps with young top boy Jamie is an eye-opener because these two characters would never normally meet in their very separate worlds, let alone have sex. Lizzie calls the shots and insists their relationship is about nothing more than physical satisfaction. This leaves Jamie looking vulnerable, almost heartbroken as he morphs back into being the teenager he really is.

Then Lizzie is kidnapped and kept at a rundown house by Dushane and Sully as part of their impending feud with top boy rivals Jamie and Modie. All-out war is fast approaching on the Summerhouse Estate.

Lizzie shows her vulnerability when she's forced to set a trap for Jamie. For the first time it appears Lizzie does have feelings for "fuck buddy" Jamie after all.

It's clear from the final scenes of series three that both of them will return to *Top Boy* series four with pivotal roles.

Other characters also seem to have backstories steeped in the real underworld.

JOE

In *Top Boy*'s early episodes, Dushane's most surprising friendship is with elderly Irish criminal Joe, played by veteran Scottish actor David Hayman.

Initially Joe is the menacing, shadowy figure supplying cocaine to old-school criminal Bobby Raikes, who provides Dushane and Sully with their food shipments for the Summerhouse Estate. In the real underworld, characters like Joe are often cold, clinical criminals whose only driving motivation is money.

Joe himself is eventually robbed and shot by the Albanians as he picks up a big shipment of drugs. But despite this, Dushane remains calm and doesn't even blame Joe for the drugs being stolen.

Then – with Joe mortally wounded in a hospital bed – Dushane visits him and talks to him like he is a father figure. It's a classic example of what can happen to those brought up without a father – they seek out emotional substitutes.

Then Joe drops completely out of the picture and some very dangerous characters begin circling.

One of them is so chilling, he's been compared by many *Top Boy* fans to a classic James Bond-type villain.

MODIE

Many who watch *Top Boy* recognise similarities between the characters and real-life London criminals. One of the standout gangsters from series three is jailed top boy Modie – played in series three with great skill by rapper Dave, aka Dave Omoregie.

One-eyed Modie is obsessed with getting out of prison and taking back his drug business from Jamie, as well as crushing rivals Dushane and Sully.

Modie eventually goes on the run from prison and returns to east London with all guns blazing, only to be gunned down by armed police who stop his car in the middle of east London.

It's similar to the way that the police shot dead real criminal Starrish Mark Duggan back in 2011, which then helped spark the Tottenham riots.

Modie's character is also like a throwback to the most frightening old-school Yardies, many of whom suffered from similar physical defects often caused by bullet wounds during shootouts with the police and rival gangsters.

He certainly behaves as if he's related to one by threatening death to everyone he meets.

One *Top Boy* fan explained: "Modie's a badass James Bond-type villain from the ghetto. We don't have time to find any redeeming characteristics in him before he goes out in a hail of bullets."

Twisted top boy Modie's influence on Sully's cousin Jermaine is there for all to see.

JERMAINE

In the real world of street gangs, revenge is a dish served at any temperature you care to desire. It's rarely put to one side.

In *Top Boy*, Jermaine – played by music producer Ashley Thomas – starts off in series one being kidnapped and almost killed by his cousin Sully.

By the time we get to series three, Jermaine is working with psycho Modie and top boy wannabe Jamie to knock Dushane and Sully off their perch. And naturally Jermaine is out for revenge on Sully for kidnapping him.

However, there are even some characters in *Top Boy* who don't deserve any of the murderous fallback that crashes down on so many of those who come from this twisted netherworld.

GEM

Young Gem – played by actor Giacomo Mancini – spends most of his time on the Summerhouse Estate during series one of *Top Boy* with his beloved dog, Marnie. He is an outsider as far as the local crew is concerned.

Gem's father is a single parent. Gem wants to know more about his mother but his father will not tell him anything, just like so many kids across the world, not just London.

Gem's only truly safe place is a tatty secret den under a railway arch. It's where he and Marnie can retreat to get away from the street gangsters on the Summerhouse Estate.

But Gem's determination to stay away from the gangs leads to him being labelled a rat because in the *Top Boy* world – both real and imagined – crews don't trust kids who won't join their clan.

When Gem's dog is killed by Dushane's soldiers because they wrongly suspect Gem of being an informant, the only person to show any real sympathy towards Gem is Chantelle, who works the corners for top boys Dushane and Sully's crew.

She tries to console Gem but at the end of series one Gem reluctantly moves out of Summerhouse with his father and they head for the Kent coastal resort of Ramsgate.

Gem re-emerges in series three in Ramsgate. But Gem's six years older than he was when he left Summerland. Now he's a classic junkie and desperate to earn some p's.

Gem represents the vicious circle of life that befalls so many of those brought up on real housing estates. Even when you think you've escaped the gangs' evil influence they come back to haunt you.

JASON

The ongoing problem of drug-addicted parents in the real world of street gangs is perfectly represented by misguided, mistreated teenager Jason – played by Ricky Smarts. He is the perfect foil to damaged top boy Sully in many ways.

Jason's crackhead mother is facing eviction, so he ends up fleeing to the south coast with his friend Sully, who relates to him because he had a mother just like that himself.

Jason is in many ways a reflection of Sully as a child and his character helps the audience understand more about Sully's damaged life.

But ultimately, Sully unintentionally becomes Jason's personal and twisted grim reaper because people who hang with Sully usually end up turning to stone.

ANCILLARY CHARACTERS

Series one of *Top Boy* was ground breaking in many respects and helped lay the groundwork for its subsequent success. But many of the characters from that first series did not reappear in subsequent episodes.

Given that one of this book's goals is to explain *Top Boy*'s relevance to the real world, it's worth noting how the experiences of those characters reflect on so many aspects of this twisted underworld.

Schoolboy and Summerland Estate resident Ra'Nell – played by Malcolm Kamulete – helped his ailing mum Lisa to get through appalling mental health problems.

Like so many growing up on housing estates, Ra'Nell has seen way too much for his tender years. He stabbed his father Wayne in the leg to stop him beating up his mother, Lisa. She is riddled with guilt about what happened, even though it was not his fault.

Lisa – played by Sharon Duncan-Brewster – suffers a form of post-traumatic stress disorder after that attack by husband Wayne.

On London's real estates, there are many thousands of children looking after themselves because their parents can't cope and a lot of those kids will end up joining a gang.

Heather – played by Kierston Wareing – is an old friend and neighbour of Lisa's. She's pregnant, single and determined to get away from the Summerhouse Estate to give her baby a better start in life than she had.

But she risks everything by growing a big crop of marijuana in her flat to sell it wholesale to her Vietnamese patron Vincent, in order to get a deposit for a home in a better area.

Then there's Leon – played by Nicholas Pinnock – who works at a mental health facility as a fitness trainer where Ra'Nell's mother Lisa is admitted after a breakdown. Leon hopes he can give her the inspiration to move on with her life, put violent husband Wayne behind her and be there for her son.

But Leon's caring nature will ultimately seal his own fate in tragic circumstances.

THE SUMMERHOUSE STORY

Balance is the key factor when it comes to so many aspects of *Top Boy*'s plotlines. The show strives to appeal to audiences way beyond the inner city.

As one fan explained: "This is a drama that is relevant to so many of us, whether we're kids, parents or grandparents. It's first and foremost about relationships from the best to the worst and that's why people can't stop watching it."

And right at the centre of it all is Summerhouse. However, many viewers of *Top Boy* will be surprised to learn that this gritty drama is deliberately located on a housing estate that doesn't actually exist.

It's closest influence is a real-life 1960s-built estate in Hackney called De Beauvoir. This has been used as a filming location on occasions but it only provides a vague backdrop for the drama.

The producers even switched in series three to using other housing estates on the outskirts of London for exterior scenes, including one in Thanet, Kent.

In fact, it can be revealed that the programme makers have an obligation to "water down" any awkward coincidences that might lead any real-life characters to presume they were being in any way identified in the series. Such legal compliance issues are of paramount importance in today's corporate TV world.

Also, *Top Boy*'s storylines are often so close to real life that the producers are obliged to make sure there are no legal comebacks from any "real-life overlaps" that might have inspired the plots and characters featured on the show.

As one *Top Boy* insider explained: "The series thrives on its 'authentic feel', which has been one of the key reasons for its success. The audience needs to believe in the characters and the plotlines, so it's inevitable that some real-life residents of housing estates might feel their stories are being told in *Top Boy*, even though this is not the case."

So far, *Top Boy* has not been sued by anyone claiming that characters in the programme are based on them. However, the show's team of legal advisors continues to work around the clock reading scripts and checking footage before, during and after production of the programme to ensure this will never happen.

As one member of the *Top Boy* crew explained: "If someone sued the programme, the entire production could be shut down. That would also mean re-filming scenes and changing plotlines, which could cost Netflix a fortune."

The fact this hasn't happened is a credit to the professionalism of the programme's writers, producers and directors.

As a result, many inside the TV industry believe *Top Boy* will go on to be one of the longest running crime series in UK television history.

And that means developing the storylines and characters with extreme care and attention.

FEELING IT

When series three of *Top Boy* was aired in 2019, Dushane and Sully had evolved into being old-school crime vets. And they had no choice but to crack down on the young hoods threatening their seat of power on the Summerhouse Estate.

But like so many seasoned street gangsters I've met, they know this can't go on for ever. The money doesn't buy them happiness but many are committed to supporting family and they don't want to let them down.

So the goalposts are constantly changing: a pivotal moment in series three comes when Dushane and Sully are in a club together but neither of them wants to even dance with a girl, let alone get high. They're looking and feeling old and worn out. They don't even approve of people taking drugs in their presence.

This is the reality of what happens when you grow up in a lawless, brutal society where the man with the biggest gun or knife wipes out all his enemies. In the end, there is a sense of "this isn't worth it".

Dushane and Sully seem to long for some sense of security and maybe that's why they keep revisiting certain places over and over again.

THE CAFF

One shouldn't forget that many street gangsters have grown up in areas of London once dominated by some of the most notorious old-fashioned British criminals of yesteryear.

Kano – who plays Sully – writes about all this in his highly acclaimed "This is England" track. He even mentions old-school criminals like the Kray Twins, as well as fond references to cups of tea, jellied eels and fry-up breakfasts.

"This is England where you can be a villain or a victim
[...] The have-nots and the have-less."

Kano has admitted he's caught in the middle of respecting the Englishness of it all but also hating it at the same time.

A number of *Top Boy*'s standout scenes take place in a typical old-fashioned workman's caff in east London that sums up that connection between today's cold-blooded young street gangsters and the old-school villains of yesteryear.

The caff is a place where Dushane and Sully seem to feel safe, because it is filled with people of all backgrounds and races. A sort of mini-melting pot in a world full of madness.

In series three's dramatic finale, young wannabe top boy Jamie even insists on making all the street gangsters a cup of tea in the middle of one of the most tense scenes.

Then Jamie is summoned to the same caff for a meeting with Dushane and Sully, who're about to go to war with him and his psychotic, on-the-run boss Modie.

As they wait for Jamie in the cafe, Sully questions Dushane as to whether any of it has been worth it.

Sully asks: "You always trying to get to the top. What for?"

Dushane looks shocked. He's become so focused on winning every war he seems to have completely lost perspective.

He doesn't really know how to answer that question.

SNAKES AND PUSSIES

The language of the street gangs is often deliberately provocative and there is no doubt it has played a huge part in sparking some deadly feuds.

Top Boy has focused a number of times on two of the most emotive words used in London's real street gang underworld which have sparked bouts of violence.

"Pussy" is a derogatory term which implies cowardice. It has a profound effect on street gangs on London's real-life inner-city Summerhouse-type housing estates, although the word itself has been used by mobsters of all shapes and sizes since the 1970s.

One former street gang member explained: "If you get called a pussy that's fuckin' insulting. It's a word that can kick off fights which have ended in knives and guns being used.

"Being in a crew is all about respect and honour and if someone calls you a pussy, they're breaking both those codes."

As war breaks out towards the end of series three, Sully and Dushane decide they have no choice but to end Dris's life after they realise he's the snake who told Sully's cousin Jermaine all about their movements.

That word "snake" is also used over and over again to remind street crews what will happen if they talk to the wrong people.

One former street gangster explained: "We're not snakes. We keep our mouths shut, even if we face decades in prison if convicted. This reminds crews that we would never inform on them. We are men to be trusted."

EAT THAT ONE, BLUD

There are constant threats lurking on every street in gang territory. It's why real street gangsters so often choose to shoot first and ask questions later.

For there are few hiding places when it comes to these closely knit crime-ridden communities.

Top Boy has reflected this by mastering the art of surprising its audience while at the same time making sure that the action is believable enough to constantly engage viewers.

In series three, Sully's cousin Jermaine bumps into Sully for the first time since Sully kidnapped and almost killed Jermaine in series one. Not surprisingly, Jermaine is out for revenge.

But Sully's response is bland and cold. "You gonna have to eat that one, blud."

In other words, swallow your pride. But you can see from the look in Jermaine's eyes that he's not going to do that.

GOMORRAH

In the real world of street gangs, many crew members will tell you they believe one particular drama series besides *Top Boy*'s cinematic "cousin" *Bullet Boy* has helped to inspire the hit TV show.

They're talking about the Italian Netflix crime drama *Gomorrah*, which is located on a housing estate in Naples, southern Italy. It's been turned into a drug-dealing netherworld by cold blooded street gangsters who somehow retain a warmth and charm, despite all the death and destruction.

One *Top Boy* fan explained: "*Gomorrah* and *Top Boy* are a template for each other when it comes to dramas about life inside young criminal gangs. Both shows taught me that it doesn't matter how alien and dangerous the world you're watching is portrayed, if it has the heart and soul it will pull an audience in."

Top Boy's premier character Dushane is similar in many ways to *Gomorrah*'s Ciro. They both have a distant soul that occasionally comes to the surface, which enables them to charm audiences. Yet they both commit some of the most appalling killings ever seen on television. In *Gomorrah*, gang leader Ciro cold-bloodedly murders a ten-year-old child. Yet the audience remain captivated by him afterwards and follow his every move.

The council estates of *Gomorrah* and *Top Boy* have a lot more in common, too. They're enclosed, rundown residential communities which encapsulate the feeling of being trapped in a world of crime and retribution.

Gomorrah's street gangsters glide through the narrow, cobbled streets of Naples on scooters while the top boys and their soldiers are either on foot inside Summerhouse or patrolling the wider, urban streets in their almost-new BMWs.

HOLLYWOOD'S GANGSTER WORLD

There are also other TV and film influences which have helped shape *Top Boy* into what it has become today.

The movies *Scarface* starring Al Pacino, *Layer Cake* with James Bond's Daniel Craig and *The Sopranos* TV series are the shows London street gangsters seem to most look up to.

One former gang member told me: "They epitomise what happens when your criminal life goes out of control."

In *Scarface*, the full, bloody reality of the Colombian cocaine invasion of 1980s Miami is laid bare. Two thousand and four's *Layer Cake* is about a drug dealer wheeling and dealing his way through London. It even gets a mention in one of *Top Boy* star Kano's rap sounds.

However, *The Sopranos* is the standout drama for the majority of gangsters. Mob boss Tony Soprano even goes to therapy to deal with issues from his childhood that revolve around his mother but never truly accepts his criminal activities have impacted on his mental health.

"A lot of these street gangsters are like that, too," said one behavioural therapist, who specialises in prison inmates. "In many ways they're surprisingly sensitive characters, despite the cold-blooded nature of their criminal lives. But they seem, like Tony Soprano, to have this ability to separate their personal lives from their professional ones most of the time."

TV mob boss Tony Soprano tries to maintain a domestic life as a typical suburban father of two by attending sports events and hosting barbecues with his family and even neighbours.

The urge to be normal seems to help shape a street gangster's life more than anything else.

"But of course their two worlds will always collide in the end," added the therapist.

LOOKING AHEAD

But what of *Top Boy*'s own TV future? How is it likely to evolve? And what can we expect from the next, much anticipated series due to be aired late in 2020?

Confirmation of the next series of *Top Boy* dropped early in 2020 after Jamie actor Michael Ward teased a picture of the show's brand new screenplay on Instagram with the words: "Killing No Murder" scrawled across the front.

Shooting of the new series was supposed to go ahead in May 2020. But at the time of writing the producers, cast and crew were on standby to start filming as soon as full coronavirus lockdown restrictions were lifted.

Top Boy star Ashley Walters had originally wanted the producers to film two seasons at the same time in early 2019, which would have worked well because of the recent coronavirus pandemic. But it was not to be.

DOMINANT FORCES

Overshadowing the next instalment of *Top Boy* as well as the real world of London street gangs will be a familiar dark, sinister force who continue to change the face of the city's underworld.

There is no doubt the Albanians will make a serious dent in series four of the TV drama as well as inside London's real narcotic business. There is no way the Eastern Europeans are going to stand back while street gangsters like top boys Dushane and Sully or their real-life equivalent try to take over London's drugs underworld.

Then there are the police. Expect them to have a much bigger role in series four of *Top Boy* as well as on the actual streets of the UK capital. They know it's high time they started to turn the screw on the young street gangsters and their drug baron paymasters.

The police can no longer sit back and watch all this death and destruction on the streets and housing estates of London. *Top Boy* will introduce a new streetwise female chief of detectives to target Dushane and Sully. And London's police probably need to take a leaf out of the TV show's book. No doubt "undies squads" of undercover detectives will be stepped up in a bid to crack down on the top boy underworld.

Obviously nothing is certain to happen. But London's police know only too well that street gangs thrive on unfinished business. The gangsters can't help hitting back hard but this may well leave them vulnerable to a counter-attack by law enforcement.

No wonder the thin line between TV drama and real-life street gangsterdom remains so blurred.

ENDLINES

I pray death don't come for me but if it does
I'll be in good company.

GHETTS AND RUDE KID, "LEGENDS DON'T DIE"

Top Boy has helped open its audience's eyes to the dark, hidden real world of poverty, violence and drug dealing that has long existed among many of London's most disaffected communities.

It's a groundbreaking series because it's British crime drama with a real difference. It's introduced depth and sensitivity to characters that had previously been unseen.

But more importantly, *Top Boy* "spoke" to an entire generation of otherwise under-represented multicultural young people growing up in the inner-city.

As a result, it's become an authentic reference point from which to draw creative inspiration and empowerment.

One of the most redeeming character traits of all the main players in *Top Boy* is that none of them think they're invincible, even when they're raking in vast amounts of cash from drugs, as well as firing guns in all directions.

These complex personalities have a sense of doom when it comes to the future. It's almost as if they know they're destined to die young and that they could have done much more with their lives. All this has undoubtedly been influenced by the real world of street gangs.

One crew member told me: "No amount of p's can water down the sadness most of us feel. I just hope the young people watching TV's *Top Boy* get the message loud and clear that being a gangster is a one-way trip to the morgue.

"A lot is always being said about these gangsters not caring if they live or die. That's crap. These kids might shrug their shoulders and make out they're hard but they don't want to die. No one does."

Drug wars on city streets featuring armed gangsters are obviously the action-driven fuel that helps to ignite *Top Boy* as a television drama.

But many fans believe that *Top Boy*'s biggest strength in depth is its "relatable" storylines. One fan explained: "Good TV drama is all about suspending disbelief. In other words, the audience has to believe in the plausibility of a story and its characters, even if there are multiple deaths and all sorts of other chilling stuff going on around it."

Meanwhile, there are some real criminals out there who've turned their lives around and are now helping kids avoid falling into the same twisted lives they once led. The real "dose of reality" side of street gangs might even help make London a safer place in the long term.

However it won't be easy. The stark reality is that most real street gangsters are more frightening than any of the characters featured in the TV series.

Real top boys don't hesitate to order their soldiers to carry out killings and beatings, which are then used as warnings to those tempted to step out of line.

And there are still a lot of teenagers out there prepared to pull triggers for money or grudges. To some of them it's as formidable as playing for a premiership football club or being a prize fighter. Some believe these street gangs remain the street equivalent of showbiz.

THE BUZZ

Old-school bank robbers from the 1970s and 1980s frequently and openly proclaimed they could never replicate the buzz they felt as they pulled off classic "blaggings" on London's streets back in the day.

Today's real top boys and their crews don't often like sharing their internal emotions or thoughts with anyone. But a lot of the ones I've spoken to do concede that they thrive on a similar "buzz" of crime.

But of course they're primarily focused on earning the p's because the clinical, greedy side of crime always takes priority over all other issues.

Today's real top boys have undoubtedly broken all the rules and fuelled a million feuds and countless murders. These men and women feeding poverty-stricken housing estates with a constant supply of drugs don't just want to steal an apple from a tree: they want to burn the orchard down as well.

That makes them the archetypal scavengers in a sense, always on the lookout for an opportunity. Drugs have provided them with a lucrative business and most don't even see themselves as being in the wrong.

GUILTLESS

"Sorry" is not a word that street gangsters often use. A lot of the ones I've met consider it a vulnerable response in a moment of weakness, which they'd later regret saying.

Freud said that if a baby had power, it would destroy the world from the frustration of its infantile desires. In some ways, these street gangsters are like those proverbial babies. Breaking the law makes them feel superior to everyone around them. It's the fuel that helps them get through life.

But the rules of their "game" are constantly being challenged.

For even in these drug-fuelled environments there is a professional structure surrounding everything. Codes and rank within the street gangs are obeyed to the letter, otherwise guns and knives will come out.

Being in a street gang is undoubtedly a reaction against feelings of inadequacy. Many of the street gangsters I've interviewed for this book even say that if they'd had more self-knowledge when they were younger, then they wouldn't have struck out so forcefully for a life of crime.

But now, embedded in this underworld, most feel alienated from so-called "normal society".

Ultimately, the real top boys and their street crews deserve little respect, especially when you look at the corpses they've left behind and the lives they've helped destroy down the years.

As one retired street gangster told me recently: "It's a shit world out there. Stuff's happening that shouldn't ever happen. It's bang, bang and you're dead time. But it's gotta end one day."

Meanwhile crime continues to thrive in the poorest areas of our society, while the spider's web of drugs starts slowly spreading beyond the traditional territories.

NEW CRIME THREATS

As global financial meltdowns and pandemics impact on us all, London's street gangs will find themselves having to push deeper and deeper into so-called safer areas of the city because those who live in more deprived areas lack the cash to buy drugs as regularly as they did before coronavirus struck.

This will lead to increasing numbers of innocent people being hurt or killed as London's drug wars spread across all neighbourhoods.

Some police officers I've spoken to recently are convinced there will be a steep increase in crimes such as kidnapping as the London underworld looks to maintain profits in spite of the long-term financial depression caused by the pandemic.

This will lead to more street gangsters emerging from the shadows as the depleted, poorly paid police struggle to maintain law and order.

So with drug prices fluctuating and other more traditional underworld enterprises such as people smuggling and prostitution also suffering because of the global crisis, the richest criminals will be looking around for new, lucrative targets.

Yet despite all this, London's so-called "black economies" will most likely continue to thrive. For even in allegedly civilised societies like Britain, illicit cash helps keep many citizens and legitimate businesses afloat.

So the real top boys and their crews will make their own twisted contribution to this nation's economy. The corner shops on numerous housing estates rely on customers who earn their keep from this illegal economy, which often provides local residents with enough cash to spend in those same stores.

In a perfect world, criminals would have no crimes to commit and everyone would live in peace and harmony. But the gap between the rich and poor is going to get even wider over the next few years.

And as the world becomes gripped by increasing poverty and unemployment, the street gangs will find it even easier to recruit more members.

DRUGLANDS

No doubt, some will accuse this book of glorifying the real street criminals and their wars. That is certainly not my intention but why should the lawlessness that exists on so many people's doorsteps today be denied?

Others may well accuse me of exaggerating the depth of the problem. But I can assure you this book portrays the tip of the underworld iceberg because this type of crime taints not only London's inner-city streets, but many other cities across the nation.

So real top boys will continue to consolidate their power and influence within the London underworld.

"The business of crime thrives on other people's misfortunes," said one retired street gangster. "We'll survive as long as people need the escapism of drugs."

These days law enforcement agencies are more reluctant to get in among the criminals in the way they tried to before most of the top boys and their crews mentioned here were even born.

Budgets, politics and so-called ethics have all played their role in changing the rules of the crime game. But the end, results for these same gangsters are high profit, low risk and few arrests.

Cocaine is currently London's second most popular recreational drug, after cannabis, with well over one million regular users in the UK capital. Street prices vary from £30 to £100 per gram. That cocaine has been "stepped on" more than anywhere else in the world to such an extent that it often only contains 5 per cent of real product.

Most of this cocaine is initially purchased wholesale from Colombian cartels for around £1,500 a kilo. The same drug, cut and sold in the UK will fetch at least £100,000 a kilo. As one cocaine baron told me: "It's been a fuckin' gold rush for years, mate. There's nothing like coke when it comes to good, old-fashioned profit."

Figures released by HM Revenue & Customs show that more than 4,000kg of cocaine was seized in the UK in 2018, an increase of more than 20 per cent over the previous four years. Yet at least 50,000kg of cocaine still slips into the UK every year, through this nation's supposedly "airtight" borders.

Meanwhile out on London's mean streets the homicide rate has – in the past five years – increased by more than 50 per cent. The majority of victims aged between sixteen and twenty-four. Nearly all of them linked to gangs and drugs.

In 2019, street murders included more than sixty stabbings, ten shootings and in one case, even involved a knife *and* a gun.

Recent freedom of information requests by journalists revealed that almost half of murder victims and murder suspects in the capital are still young black men. This is way out of proportion to the demographics of London's current population – which is just 13 per cent black.

This is also in stark contrast to elsewhere in the UK, where the racial and age profile of murder victims and suspects much more precisely reflects the inhabitants of those areas.

MAKING A DENT

Many will doubtless argue, on almost Marxist terms, that "society has the drugs underworld it deserves". In other words, society created these drugs, so what's the problem?

Street gangsters relish the relative fame that comes with their "jobs". Drugs have created a hunger that is unstoppable.

Fromm, in his *Anatomy of Human Destructiveness*, called it: "The need to make a dent."

On London's housing estates, few of these street criminals care about the future. They have spent years being controlled by other more powerful criminals and a lot of them are saying "Now it's our turn to run things".

So when Dushane double-crosses white old-school criminal Bobby Raikes and kills him at point blank range, there would have been few in the audience upset by that murder.

One former street crew member from north London explained: "When Dushane popped Raikes there would have been a round of applause or two because people like him had been running things for far too long back in 2011 when series one was first aired."

ON A HIGH

One must never forget that many real street gangsters find it hard to cope with their lives of crime unless they neutralise themselves by taking drugs to kill the pain.

Narcotics have long been renowned as a way to ease long bouts of boredom and depression. But this often in turn leads to more crimes being committed. It's the ultimate vicious circle. Although many would deny it, a lot of street gangsters who deal in drugs also take them.

A lot of street gangsters also rely on the high of drugs to give them the courage to commit crimes to get them through the difficult times. It's all part of their own never-ending quest for survival.

And of course drugs also help encourage them to hit back at society because they feel they owe it nothing.

There is a comparison to be made between *Top Boy* and the books of Charles Dickens because of the way the TV series skilfully explains to the audience why these people sell drugs and commit crimes, often in order to feed their poverty-stricken families.

One TV producer explained: "The only way to ensure an audience can engage in a world that is so alien to many of them is to provide some answers before anyone asks the questions. *Top Boy* does that superbly."

Top Boy also continually asks the question: "Why? Why are people obliged to live in cramped concrete jungles? Why do they choose a life of crime ahead of everything else?"

Some would say the answers to this lie in people's upbringings, especially the ones with childhoods run by single mothers.

MUM'S THE WORD

Rapper Kano – who plays Sully in *Top Boy* – sums up the unenviable role of the mothers of many street gangsters when he says in one of his best loved tracks, "Trouble":

"All of our mothers worry when we touch the road,
'cause it's touch and go, whether we're coming home."

In *Top Boy* there's a scene where a mother assures her son's concerned teacher that he is not a street gangster by saying: "A mother knows her child."

That phrase perfectly sums up the response of real-life mothers whose sons are caught up in street gangs in London and across many of the UK's major cities.

Some of these mothers may well know the uncomfortable truth about their sons' criminal habits. But it's tough to face the reality that your loved one is a cold-blooded gangster. Much easier perhaps to live in a state of complete denial, which can often help to save face in front of other people within the community and avoid vicious gossip and insinuation a lot of the time.

One child behavioural therapist explained: "In a sense, these mothers are enabling their sons to continue being criminals by not confronting them about their gangster lives."

Real-life street gangsters I've spoken to rarely want to recognise this type of character development. But one former crew member told me: "Our mums so often bear the brunt of everything. As a result, they're overprotective and many sons take full advantage of this by lying about their criminal activities to their mums, so as to not hurt their feelings and disappoint them."

Some behavioural experts believe that mothers of street gangsters should take more responsibility for their child's actions. One explained: "I fully appreciate a mother's bond to her child, especially her son, is to protect them at all costs. But they need to take some responsibility for nurturing these children and sending them in the wrong direction.

"Sure, these mothers show incredible strength and loyalty but they're unintentionally sanctioning their sons' criminal lives, without ever facing up to the consequences of their actions."

In the real world, there is little support available to help mothers and their sons break out of this endless cycle, which is so often sparked by adverse childhood experiences.

Naturally, some London street gangsters thrive on all the trappings of wealth and the excitement of being a risk-taking criminal. But a few I've encountered actually long to lead normal lives so they can be honest to their mothers and switch off being a criminal and enjoy a safe and law-abiding life, or so they think.

As the same behavioural expert added: "Having an absent father doesn't give you an excuse to start murdering people."

WRONG PATH

Some street gangsters I've encountered project a narrative that their poverty-stricken childhood forced them into a life of crime. They are also convinced that being a criminal will provide them with a good income and respect from their peers.

Obviously, the police look at all this very differently. One recently retired gang liaison officer told me: "Being born poor with a single parent is no excuse. These kids make choices.

But the saddest thing about it all is that so often the gangsters themselves are highly intelligent and you think to yourself: 'Why oh why didn't they stay on at school, get some qualifications and try and make it in the real world?'"

But many street gangsters remain convinced it's ingrained in them. One said: "When you grow up on an estate and the only kids who seem to have a good time are the gangsters, it gets right under yer skin.

"It just doesn't seem fair to you, so you start wondering what it might be like to have a flash car and not have to worry about paying the bills. Then you see some of them with the prettiest girls on their arms and you start to get jealous. You want a piece of all that for yourself.

"Then one day you get stopped and searched by some nasty feds and you think, 'What's the point of being honest? They're gonna give you a kickin' anyway, so you might as well make some p's and stick two fingers up at them.'"

And avoiding the gangster life to enjoy a safe and law-abiding life is even less likely once you've crossed that line.

COPING MECHANISM

It's too easy to make the overriding theme of this book that broken families mean broken lives. It's really not as simple as that in real life.

Some child behavioural experts are convinced it's not what happens to someone during their childhood that matters. It's how they respond afterwards to what they've experienced.

In other words, a person's coping mechanism often contributes more to this than what they actually went through during childhood. Some people turn bad experiences into empowering events and use them to forge their way through life.

Others get "stuck" or "frozen" and find that the bad memories and influences never go away. This gives them an excuse or a "licence" for what happens to them later in life. It's a deadly cycle that legitimises criminal activities in the mind of many street gangsters.

In other words, people were brutal to them during their childhoods, so they don't believe they owe society anything. As a result, they will do what the fuck they want and no one can stop them.

BACK TO REALITY

Some social housing experts say the only way to end the gang domination of many London estates is to knock all the tower blocks down and rebuild them as low-rise homes.

But it really isn't as simple as that.

As one planning expert explained: "The trouble is, there is a national housing shortage crisis, so if we only built low-rise there wouldn't be enough homes to go round. We need more homes, not less."

Shortly after completing this book, I got a phone call from one of the street gangsters I'd interviewed in London. His crew had taken a pounding from the police and rival crews during the first couple of months of 2020. Then along came the coronavirus lockdown and the streets emptied overnight.

The last straw for this street gangster came when a car he was driving was shot up by what he thought were rival gangsters. One of his crew was seriously injured as he scrambled under his car and played dead.

This street gangster heard that the Albanians were behind it. They'd decided to have him taken out as a lesson to other street gangs to fall in line following a territorial dispute.

"I hadn't done nothing," he explained. "They just thought it was time to tell everyone that they was still in charge.

"I was stunned and for the first time I actually questioned what I was doin' in this game. I could have been killed, even though I'd done nothing wrong."

The Albanians eventually called off the hit because they felt the original shooting had sent enough of a message to their street gangsters without actually having to kill someone to prove their point.

"I knew then that I had to get out, but it's easier said than done," the same street gangster explained. "I'm still trying to work out how to do it without anyone coming after me because they don't like you leaving this game, ever.

"Remember, you're also the keeper of the gang's secrets. If you talk about it to anyone outside, then you could endanger a lot of people's lives."

This gangster had these words of advice for any youth living on an inner-city housing estate trying to get into the drug business.

"Don't do it, bruv. This is hell on earth. Once you're in, you'll struggle to get out alive. I've got a death sentence hanging over me, even though I done nothing wrong. Head for the normal world and lead a happy, safe life. You won't regret it."

EPILOGUE

JONSON ROAD, STEPNEY GREEN,
EAST LONDON: 13 MARCH 2020

Shocking footage from a video posted on social media captures a gang of youths stamping on a man and hitting him over the head as he lies on the road in broad daylight.

Eventually the man curls up on the floor to try and avoid the kicks and punches reigning down on him. He's surrounded by at least six people.

They aggressively stamp on him while another youth steps forward and starts smashing him over the head with what appears to be a golf club.

A woman intervenes in the brawl, attempting to stop one of the attackers, before another man helps and chases them away.

One of the attackers shouts at the man lying on the ground writhing in agony.

Other members of the public attend to the victim, who seems dazed. He eventually stands up and walks off down the road.

Moments later, the victim takes off a satchel he was wearing the whole time and passes it to another man, who then hands it to another gang member as they all walk away.

The food is more important than anything else...

JUST HANGING ON

Back at that same east London housing estate I described in the opening of this book, nothing much has changed. The real top boys and their crews still dominate the walkways, corridors and alleyways of this concrete jungle.

The corner crews are still out selling pills, coke, speed and puff to all comers. The kids still hide food in their mouths if the police make a rare appearance. They still spit it out to sell to customers in exchange for some p's.

The same deadly feuds are erupting into violence every few weeks and most residents remain as scared as ever of encountering the criminals who run this estate and many others like it across London.

One mother's son was shot and killed here early in 2020. Now she and this boy's siblings face terror on a daily basis from the same gangsters they suspect of killing their loved one.

This mother summed it all up: "It's there all the time and you have to face the fact that if your child hadn't mixed with certain people he'd still be alive. It makes it hurt even deeper. Living here, in the place where he died, and knowing people are shielding his killer is so hard to handle."

The mother and her surviving children are trapped in a dark web of evil that's represented by the estate where they live. They can see the hooded young gangsters they believe are responsible for murder from the windows of their flat as they loiter on the walkways and alleys below them.

This family also has to contend with a never-ending rumour mill about how the victim – their loved one – deserved what happened to him because he was once a member of the gang those murderous youths belong to.

The same mother explained: "Every day you walk past kids who at least know who the killer was. Then you look up and catch their eye and you realise that could be the person who murdered your own child. The pain is unbearable. Sure, we feel anger, but most of all we are drained by it all. We just don't know which way to turn.

"You go to the shops and there they are yet again leaning against a wall. You want to confront them but you know it could cost you your life or that of another member of your family."

In one scene on *Top Boy*, Dushane is shown trying to deal sympathetically with a murder victim's family but at no point does he look truly remorseful. It's as if there's a psychological barrier preventing Dushane from showing real emotion because that might be seen as a sign of weakness.

A former street gangster I know called Dino explained: "The makers of *Top Boy* need to show even more clearly the devastation that comes from a cold-blooded gang murder. But they also have to continue to convey the hardness of the top boys and how they brush off what they have done. It's a difficult balancing act."

Meanwhile, in the concrete tower blocks of London's deprived inner-city housing estates, many yungers continue pushing for membership of street gangs, despite the horror stories on their doorsteps and the scenes dressed up as drama on *Top Boy*. To many, gang membership remains their ultimate ambition.

They've been fed never-ending war stories about cocaine, robberies, violence, killings and the inter-gang rivalry that keys into their own twisted aspirations.

You can't even blame drill rappers for telling the world how these gangsters shot down their enemies. In fact, these days many performers have watered down their lyrics because they now recognise that the gangster life is a deadly one-way street.

But there are still some artists who do not change content and their songs continue to dominate YouTube and various other social media sites.

Then in the middle of all this, something happened which many believed would be the beginning of the end for the real top boys.

PANDEMIC

The recent worldwide coronavirus outbreak should have had a more damaging impact on drugs sales than any police SWAT team raids.

On the estates of London and the UK's other inner cities, the number of customers halved virtually overnight as the virus kicked in during the early spring of 2020.

According to some London social workers, the strict stay-at-home rules initially led to many reflecting in a "profound" way about their criminal lifestyles and aspirations.

The National Crime Agency also issued a statement that street crime gangs and dealers had been forced onto the back foot by the pandemic.

The UK feds claimed at least ten tonnes of Class A drugs had been seized globally since the pandemic first flared up in early March 2020.

Law enforcement officials insisted that lockdowns in countries where drugs were sourced – such as Pakistan and Colombia – had been hit by aviation and shipping bans. This caused many of the criminals who help supply the drug shipments to London street gangs to transport larger quantities in each consignment, leaving them more vulnerable to interception.

In one incident on 23 April 2020, three men were arrested after cocaine worth £3 million was found in a "purpose-built hide" in a lorry that had travelled on a ferry from France to Dover.

But then some criminologists predicted a spike in street gang murders as the coronavirus lockdown eased during the summer of 2020. Many gangs had been taunting each other on social media throughout the pandemic and once they got back on the streets, blood would be spilled.

By the start of July 2020, late-night bloc parties were being hosted on many of the very same housing estates that feature in this book. Street gangs sent their dealers in among the crowds to make a killing and it was clear that London's drug-fuelled crimelands were rapidly returning to the way they were before the pandemic.

So back on the walkways and alleys of London's housing estates, it seems the food game is very much still alive and kicking.

SPOILER ALERT

Inevitably, I will have upset future fans of *Top Boy* by mentioning some of the show's storylines here. I've tried my hardest not to give away too much. But it was impossible to write this book without doing this to a certain degree.

And to those who've already been gripped by all three series of *Top Boy* I say: Watch them all over again! It really is worth it because the show's multilayered dramatic texture helps expose new roots to the plotlines each time you watch it. In other words, sit back and enjoy the ride – again and again.

Top Boy's success owes much to its uniquely London "flavour". Creator Ronan Bennett skilfully gives the audience a glimpse into the underbelly of the city, a million miles away from the usual clichés like Big Ben and Buckingham Palace.

Many believe that this has helped the new 2019 Netflix version of the series get such a huge foothold in the global TV market.

THE REAL TOP BOYS
SOURCES/ACCESS

But what of the real top boys who took such enormous risks by contributing to this book?

Many had initially warned me that London's current crop of street gangsters would never come clean because of fears about the feds and their rivals.

So, however I word this note, I'm going to upset some of them. One of my main sources for this book put it bluntly: "There are street crews out there who'll be angry that I talked to you. They're bad men. They shoot first and ask questions later."

But I was pleasantly surprised by the level of access I managed to gain in order to tell the real top boys' story. Many criminal faces I know were amazed I managed to get any of these young street gangsters to open up.

No doubt some interviews were provided to me by hoods who couldn't resist showing off because they were desperate to be *somebody*.

Yet others I met showed a remarkable degree of humility. They're not all just cold-blooded desperados prepared to kill anyone to get what they want.

Far from it; many are lost souls, abandoned by their families at an early age and left to fend for themselves. It's not really surprising they opted for life in a gang. They had little choice.

No doubt many will try to compare the characters featured in *Top Boy* with the real gangsters and their crews mentioned in this book. But remember the real top boys are much more chilling.

Most of the true stories you've read here have been revealed by street gangsters who actually wanted their lives to be exposed on certain conditions.

I was obliged to offer them a deal: talk to me openly and honestly, and I will protect your identity by even giving you a fictional street name. I suppose you could call it a literary version of the witness protection programme.

I granted them this immunity because telling their stories is more important than knowing their real names. *Top Boy*'s TV success has also helped because it's definitely "normalised" this chilling netherworld to many law-abiding citizens.

It's also true that some criminals I encountered demanded a fee for their help. I refused to give them a penny as that would have tainted what they had to say and brought into doubt many issues.

Much easier to ignore the greedy ones and promise the others complete discretion in order for them to talk openly about sensitive information without living in fear of retribution.

These real Top Boys and their crews have perpetrated widespread and extreme acts of crime within their communities. But I can't always accurately depict those real acts of trauma in case that leads to identifying sources or innocent participants.

So, some events in this book have had to be dramatised because I didn't want to misrepresent the real stories and the suffering that people have been through in this chilling real underworld.

Obviously, there are few readily available written records covering many of the activities outlined here. That means trusting the judgement and recollections of numerous individuals, many of whom do not have their full names reproduced in this book.

As a result, much of the information in this book has been dependent on the memories of men and women – fallible, contradictory, touched by pride and capable of gross omission. However, I believe their accounts because there are no hidden agendas in their stories. I make no apologies for the strong language either.

Much of the dialogue represented in this book was constructed from available documents, some was drawn from courtroom testimony, and some was reconstituted from the memory of participants.

No doubt I've missed out a few pivotal characters in the story of the real top boys. So, to those individuals I say sorry, although I'm not sure any of them will mind!

Ultimately, I've recreated stories of street gangsters which have twisted and turned from the mean streets of London to the unlikely criminal badlands of Middle England and then back to the UK capital's urban concrete jungles.

It's been an extraordinary eye-opener and I hope you've enjoyed and relished it as much as I have.

Wensley Clarkson, London 2020

*To close the eyes, and give a seemly comfort
to the apparel of the dead, is poverty's
holiest touch of nature.*

CHARLES DICKENS